HOUSE
PLANTS

HOUSE
PLANTS

PAUL WILLIAMS

LONDON, NEW YORK, MUNICH,
MELBOURNE, DELHI

SENIOR EDITOR Helen Fewster
PROJECT ART EDITOR Rachael Smith
MANAGING EDITOR Anna Kruger
MANAGING ART EDITOR Alison Donovan
DTP DESIGNER Louise Waller
PICTURE RESEARCH Lucy Claxton, Richard Dabb,
Myriam Megharbi
EDITORIAL ASSISTANT Katie Dock
PRODUCTION CONTROLLER Sarah Sherlock

Photography by
SIAN IRVINE

First published by Dorling Kindersley Ltd in 2006
Text copyright © 2006 Paul Williams

Penguin Books Ltd, 80 Strand, London WC2R 0RL, England.

2 4 6 8 10 9 7 5 3 1

Copyright © 2006 Dorling Kindersley Limited
A Penguin Company

A CIP catalogue record for this book is available from the British Library.

ISBN 1-4503-1067-7

SD182
Colour reproduction by RGB, Italy.
Printed and bound in China by Hung Hing.

Discover more at
www.dk.com

Contents

Flowering plants

Impatiens p.104

Exacum p.83

Hibiscus p.97

Streptocarpus p.162

Justicia p.107

Saintpaulia p.146

Mandevilla p.113

Campanula p.44

Anthurium p.28

Pericallis p.132

Punica p.141

Pelargonium p.127

Abutilon p.18

Clivia p.56

Brugmansia p.38

Lantana p.110

THERE'S A HOUSEPLANT for almost every situation; this visual guide is designed to help you find one that fits your requirements quickly and easily. Whether you're looking for colourful foliage, scented flowers, something for your bathroom, conservatory, to cheer the house in winter, or a near-indistructable cactus, the Plant Chooser will point you in the right direction.

Scented flowers

Winter features

Orchids

Solanum p.153

Capsicum p.45

Lavandula p.111

Gardenia p.91

Cyclamen p.66

Rhododendron p.143

Stephanotis p.161

Jasminum p.106

Hippeastrum p.98

Schlumbergera p.149

Phalaenopsis p.133

Paphiopedilum p.125

Euphorbia pulcherrima p.81

Camellia p.43

Dendrobium p.71

Cymbidium p.67

Plant chooser | Interesting foliage

Patterned foliage

Texture

Coloured leaves

Pilea p.137

Solenostemon p.155

Nertera p.121

Gynura p.94

Ctenanthe p.62

Begonia pp.34–35

Davallia p.70

Selaginella p.151

Calathea pp.40–41

Caladium p.39

Hypoestes p.101

Hemigraphis p.96

Stromanthe p.163

Maranta p.114

Tradescantia spathacea p.167

Fittonia p.90

Dramatic shape

Codiaeum p.57

Cycas p.65

Nolina p.122

Platycerium p.138

Aechmea p.21

Euphorbia trigona p.82

Air fresheners

Ficus sagittata pp.86–87

Spathiphyllum p.160

Hedera p.95

Chlorophytum p.52

Aglaonema p.24

Dieffenbachia p.72

Syngonium p.164

Dracaena pp.76–77

Plant chooser | Plant specialities

Climbers and trailers

Epipremnum p.80

Hedera p.95

Cissus p.54

Hoya p.100

Senecio rowleyanus p.152

Passiflora p.126

Senecio macroglossus p.152

Cacti and succulents

Ferocactus p.85

Sedum p.150

Agave p.23

Echeveria p.79

Euphorbia tirucalli p.82

Aeonium p.22

Zamioculcas p.171

Aloe p.26

Large plants

Yucca p.170

Curcuma p.64

Ficus binnendijkii 'Alii' pp.86–87

Philodendron pp.134–135

Monstera p.115

Palms

Phoenix p.136

Howea p.99

Rhapis p.142

Dypsis p.78

Introduction

Most of us get satisfaction from being involved with nature in some way. Houseplants bring nature indoors, and at the same time you can take things one step further by making them important design elements in the home. There's a plant to satisfy everyone's style and taste, and the benefits are well documented: houseplants not only brighten up your interior, but they can help reduce stress, and also remove volatile chemicals from the air.

This book is a personal selection of reliable, effective plants, but it represents only a fraction of those available from florists, DIY stores, and garden centres. Once bitten by the houseplant bug you'll find plenty of others to try. Any golden rules? Take a little time to consider what conditions you have to offer and which plants will grow under those conditions and you are well on your way to having healthy, good-looking plants that take up a minimum of your time but provide maximum pleasure.

Floral displays immediately brighten up your living room, adding instant colour, and sometimes scent.

Even simple plants can become stunning and stylish design features – be inventive with your displays.

Group arrangements bring extra benefit to your indoor plants. When you position plants with similar needs in close proximity, they work together to create the right level of moisture in the air.

Just by being there, a plant can improve air quality and make your indoor environment a healthier place. The common spider plant is easy to grow and research has shown that it is particularly useful at purifying the atmosphere by filtering common household pollutants.

It's best to choose your plants to suit your site if you want them to thrive.

The range of plants available changes constantly, giving you endless scope to transform your interior.

Using this book

If you're looking for a plant with a particular feature, or for specific conditions, turn to the Plant Chooser for inspiration. There you'll find a pictorial selection, and the page reference will take you straight to the main entry. At the back there is an expanded unillustrated version of this list.

In the A–Z section you will find brief descriptions of around 150 plants, listed in alphabetical order by their botanical names. I have broken down the information into categories to help you check that the plant suits your conditions. Watering and Survival Strategy are fairly self explanatory, but some of the others contain generalisations that demand a little explanation.

Light is tricky to define without getting into the technicalities of lux ratings and light meters. There are many variables: the level is dictated by how far north or south you are, and there is a significant difference in the quality of winter and summer light. North-, south-, east- and west-facing windows all receive varying amounts of light at different strengths. Here, good light is taken to mean bright light, but not direct sun. Many plants tolerate a weaker direct morning or afternoon sun but not midday heat.

Temperature Normal room temperature is defined as 18–24°C (64–75°F). This is a general definition and many plants tolerate a few degrees either side of that range.

Size You can often buy plants in a range of sizes; some bigger than shown here, and others smaller. The measurement given on the page is the overall height of the plant and pot illustrated. Large plants are listed in the category index on pp.188–190.

Site Throughout the book I have suggested ways or places to display each plant. These examples are entirely subjective and by no means exhaustive but are offered as pointers to a suitable site, assuming the light and temperature conditions are met.

At the end of the book I have provided a short practical section offering general advice on plant care. Most plants are prone to at least one or two common pests and diseases, and these, as well as routine problems, are fully covered to help you find out what may have gone wrong, and how to put it right.

A–Z of plants

Abutilon × *hybridum*
Flowering maple

Abutilons are easy plants for cool, light
conditions. Substantial bell-shaped flowers in
a range of colours, from deep red to orange,
yellow, and pink, are produced during
summer and into autumn, and the maple-
leaf foliage has its own appeal.
A. pictum 'Thompsonii' has netted
variegated leaves; the patterning
is caused by a virus, but it is not
readily spread to other plants
and does little to slow their
vigour. Given enough
warmth, the evergreens
keep growing all year –
make sure you provide plenty of
light to satisfy any growth stimulated
by high temperatures, or your plants
will become weak, pale, and drawn.

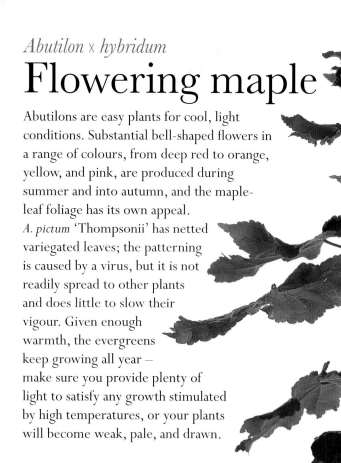

A. pictum 'Thompsonii'

HOW MUCH LIGHT
Abutilons enjoy full sun, but make
sure you keep them moist at the
roots to avoid scorching.

ROOM TEMPERATURE
Winter lows of a few degrees above
freezing will be tolerated, but cool
rooms, 16–20°C (61–68°F), are ideal.

WHEN TO WATER
In warm environments keep the
compost moist year round. If winters
are cooler, reduce the amount of
water and allow compost to dry
slightly between waterings. Provide
fortnightly doses of balanced liquid
feed when the plant is in active
growth but stop feeding in winter.

SURVIVAL STRATEGY
Keep plants within bounds by cutting
back hard in spring; if you pinch out
the growing tips at the same time,
you'll get a bushier plant, but it may
delay flowering slightly. Growth can
be vigorous in summer, so you may
need to prune again in early autumn.
Look out for whitefly (see p.187).

SIZE
55cm/22in

SITE
Conservatory;
south-facing
window

Acalypha hispida

Red-hot cat's tail

Acalyphas are bushy plants grown for their foliage and fluffy
catkins. *A. hispida* has toothed leaves and red catkins that
extend up to 40cm (16in) and appear on-and-off all summer.
The plant may grow to 1.5m (5ft) but you can keep it small
by cutting it back in spring or autumn. Speckled varieties of
A. wilkesiana, with red, green,
purple, and copper colouring,
may be an acquired taste, but
those with single-coloured
leaves and contrasting
margins are indeed
handsome.

HOW MUCH LIGHT
For good flowers and foliage colour,
provide bright, filtered light, such as
you might get through a net curtain.

ROOM TEMPERATURE
Acalyphas need a winter minimum
of 13–15°C (55–59°F). Lower night
temperatures cause leaves to drop.

WHEN TO WATER
During the period of maximum
growth keep the compost moist. In
the cooler winter months keep
plants on the drier side, but do not
allow the compost to dry out
completely.

SURVIVAL STRATEGY
Acalyphas enjoy humid conditions:
grow two or three together, or with
other plants, to help maintain high
levels of local humidity. When the
weather is particularly warm, your
plants will benefit from a regular
spray of water on their foliage.

SIZE
35cm/14in

SITE
Conservatory

Adiantum capillus-veneris

Maidenhair fern

There are several species of adiantum, all coming under the general name of maidenhair ferns, and *A. capillus-veneris* is one of the prettiest – few plants match its delicacy and grace. The arching fronds are divided into fan-shaped, pale green "pinnae" that contrast beautifully with the fine black stems that carry them. It's a useful little plant for many difficult-to-fill spaces around the home, taking low light levels and cooler positions in its stride.

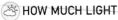
Fronds are made up of fan-shaped "pinnae" (leaflets).

HOW MUCH LIGHT
Keep out of direct sunlight but provide good filtered light.

ROOM TEMPERATURE
Normal room temperature 18–24°C (64–75°F) is sufficient, but it will tolerate as little as 10°C (50°F).

WHEN TO WATER
Keep the compost just moist throughout the year. The leaves will soon crisp if the roots become dry. The higher the temperature the greater the need for humidity.

SURVIVAL STRATEGY
Provided you keep it moist, this is an easy plant to grow. If it becomes untidy you can give your plant a manicure – and a new lease of life – by cutting off all the fronds at the base; it will soon produce a new set. Spring is the best time to do this.

SIZE
40cm/16in

SITE
Bathroom

Aechmea fasciata

Vase plant

A striking South American plant from the forest floor, whose dramatic foliage forms a natural "urn", designed to catch rain dripping from above. Its small blue flowers (which turn red) are short lived, but the bracts last a lot longer. Each rosette has just one flowerhead, but it dies back slowly: plants look good for months after flowering whilst new rosettes develop to replace old.

Showy bracts are visible for up to two months

HOW MUCH LIGHT
Good light is essential for flowering: it will tolerate a few hours of direct sunlight, but not scorching, hot sun.

ROOM TEMPERATURE
Suits winter minimum of 15°C (59°F) and summer maximum – provided humidity is high – of 27°C (81°F).

WHEN TO WATER
Keep the centre of the plant filled with soft water. Empty this out occasionally and refill it with fresh water. Keep the compost just moist during summer; in winter allow it to partially dry out before watering sparingly.

SURVIVAL STRATEGY
Despite its humid, tropical origins, it tolerates a wide range of conditions, but if it's too hot and dry, the leaf tips will go brown. Apply a half-strength balanced liquid feed fortnightly in summer. A small pot satisfies a large plant; for stability choose a clay one, or use a weighty cachepot.

SIZE
60cm/24in

SITE
Brightly lit room

Aeonium 'Zwartkop'
Aeonium

This is as near to black as you can get in a houseplant. The dramatic foliage forms fleshy rosettes at the end of bare, snake-like stems – combine it with hard steel or glass surfaces for a sharp minimalist look. Large heads of small bright yellow flowers may be produced in early summer. It is easy to grow, with no particular temperature requirements, but good light is essential. Light deficiency causes leaves to elongate and become greener, leading to open, straggly rosettes. It can take full sun, or live outside in summer. Use a heavy pot to give tall plants stability.

HOW MUCH LIGHT
Requires maximum light all year, even in winter when growth stops and plants are virtually dormant.

ROOM TEMPERATURE
Prefers cool winters, around 8–11°C (46–52°F); in summer temperatures between 18–25°C (64–77°F) suffice.

WHEN TO WATER
Keep compost moist in summer, to prevent foliage flagging. In winter, reduce watering but water if leaves drop or lose their shine. Give a half-strength balanced liquid feed every month in summer and nothing in winter. Keep water off the foliage: it leaves an unsightly white deposit.

SURVIVAL STRATEGY
Old leaves shrivel and fall: this is normal. Tall, bare-stemmed plants can be cut back hard. It takes nerve to cut most of your plant off but you will end up with a nicer shape, and you can root the rosettes you remove in moist gritty compost. Vine weevil can be a nuisance (see p.187).

SIZE
50cm/20in

SITE
Minimalist interior

Agave attenuata

Agave

Agaves are tough, strongly-shaped plants, ideal for the bright sunshine and heat of a conservatory. They make good architectural specimen plants. *A. attenuata* develops a stout trunk. The more common *A. americana* forms a rosette with broad, spiny-edged leaves which can eventually grow very large. There are also smaller, slower-growing species: *A. filifera* has wispy white threads edging its leaves, and stocky *A. victoriae-reginae*, which is no higher than 25cm (10in) and makes a compact rosette of leaves with bright white marks.

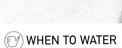 **HOW MUCH LIGHT**
Provide as much light as possible throughout the year.

ROOM TEMPERATURE
Agaves are tolerant of low winter temperatures of around 5–6°C (41–43°F) if they are kept dry.

WHEN TO WATER
During active growth water regularly making the compost moist but letting the compost partly dry out in between waterings. In winter keep just enough moisture in the compost to stop it drying completely.

SURVIVAL STRATEGY
Undemanding plants with no special needs. Some have very sharp spiny tips which can be dangerous for children's eyes – trim them off with nail clippers, or skewer wine corks on the tips. New plants are often bundled up for transport; the leaves will spread and flatten out with time.

SIZE
56cm/ 22½in

SITE
Contemporary styled interior

Aloe variegata

Partridge-breasted aloe

There are many kinds of aloe and all are easy to grow. *A. variegata* is tough and smaller than most, making it an ideal house guest. Spikes of tubular red flowers emerge in spring and early summer, but its robust foliage looks good all year. *A. vera*'s reputation as a healer ensures a welcome on windowsills across the world. It forms a rosette of upright, succulent leaves, spotted pale white with toothed edges, and produces tall spikes of yellow flowers. For even more tactile effects, try *A. aristata,* whose compact rosette is comprised of fleshy leaves dashed with knobbly tubercules, and sends up typical orange aloe flowers on 30cm (12in) stalks in summer.

A. aristata (Lace aloe)

HOW MUCH LIGHT
Aloes need good light all year round. They tolerate full sun but keep them out of very hot midday summer sun.

ROOM TEMPERATURE
Ideal range is 18–24°C (64–75°F). For flowers, provide a 4–5 week chilling – as low as 10°C (50°F) – in winter.

WHEN TO WATER
Take care to keep water out of the tightly packed foliage. In summer keep the compost just moist; in winter keep on the dry side but do not allow it to dry out completely. Apply a half-strength balanced liquid feed every 2 weeks during summer. Stop feeding in winter.

SURVIVAL STRATEGY
Aloes are easily cared for: simply provide plenty of light and ensure they are not over-watered. They often produce offsets, which you can cut off and pot up into a free-draining, loam-based compost.

SIZE
67cm/27in

SITE
Sunny windowsill

Ananas comosus var. *variegatus*

Pineapple

A striking plant that may unfortunately become too big for most homes, but it is spectacularly showy if you have the space. It's a variegated form of the edible pineapple with bold narrow leaves up to 90cm (36in) long, toothed and edged with a broad creamy-white stripe. If you have room, try combining it with other bromeliads, such as billbergias and aechmeas, to create a themed display of rich textures and dramatic shapes.

In direct sunlight, leaf margins acquire a pink tinge.

☼ HOW MUCH LIGHT
Ananas does not have a resting period so it needs as much direct sunlight as possible all year.

🌡 ROOM TEMPERATURE
Keep warm all year round, with a winter minimum of 16°C (61°F).

💧 WHEN TO WATER
A. comosus grows year round so water frequently in summer and keep the compost just moist during winter. The cooler the winter temperature, the drier the plant should be kept.

✋ SURVIVAL STRATEGY
Given a warm temperature, good light, moderate humidity, and a free-draining bromeliad compost this is a straightforward plant to care for. Unfortunately the fruit takes several months to mature and is unlikely to reach any great size or even be edible when grown indoors.

SIZE
36cm/
14½in

SITE
Conservatory

Anthurium hybrids

Flamingo flower

There are a number of species of anthurium; many are very large and usually grown as cut flowers for florists. But for the home, breeders have produced compact plants that are more tolerant of household conditions. Their shiny white, pink, or red flowers appear intermittently throughout the year, but even when out of flower they make attractive foliage plants. The flowers have a presence all of their own, so give your plant a prominent position. Anthuriums are best displayed individually in a simple but stylish pot that does not attempt to compete with the flowers.

A. 'Champion'

HOW MUCH LIGHT
Provide strong but indirect light in summer but during winter, when the sun is weaker, it will enjoy full light.

ROOM TEMPERATURE
The winter minimum is 16°C (61°F), but a year-round constant of around 20°C (68°F) is preferable.

WHEN TO WATER
A tricky customer. Never allow the compost to dry out, but also avoid a continually soggy compost, as this will damage the roots.

SURVIVAL STRATEGY
This is not the easiest plant to grow because it needs constant conditions of temperature and humidity. It will not tolerate draughts, so position it away from doors or open windows. Raise humidity by spraying regularly.

SIZE
56cm/
22½in

SITE
Bathroom

Asparagus densiflorus 'Myersii'

Foxtail fern

Despite its common name this is not a fern – although with its soft and fluffy foliage it could understandably be taken for one at first glance. It is a tough plant with large tuberous water-storing roots which give it a degree of resilience towards drying out and make it much more tolerant of heat and drought than many true ferns. A well grown plant makes a good bushy mound of light green foliage on upright stems 40cm (16in) long. It is ideal as a foil for larger leaves or as soft background for brightly flowered plants. For an elegant and slightly oriental look, consider the fine, wispy leaves and tiered stems of *A. setaceus*. Young plants are small and bushy but as they mature they reveal that their real inclination is to climb – by sending out long shoots and scrambling up to 3m (10ft) in height. If space is an issue, *A. setaceus* 'Nanus' stays small and compact.

A. setaceus

HOW MUCH LIGHT
Provide plenty of bright light but avoid direct sunlight.

ROOM TEMPERATURE
Tolerates lows of 7°C (45°F), happier at 16–21°C (61–70°F). A. setaceus needs warmer winters (13°C/55°F).

WHEN TO WATER
Water both A. densiflorus and A. setaceus regularly during summer keeping the compost continually moist but not wet. Reduce watering during winter, so compost is only just moist. If A. setaeus becomes dry, its fine leaves will quickly turn brown.

SURVIVAL STRATEGY
Undernourished plants become a pale and sickly looking green, so apply a balanced liquid feed regularly during summer. If plants become congested (or if you just want more), divide in spring by splitting apart the dense mass of tubers and potting up the divisions.

SIZE
49cm/ 19½in

SITE

Bathroom; hanging basket

Aspidistra elatior

Cast-iron plant

The aspidistra has almost become a victim of its own success: because it can withstand considerable neglect, it gets considerably neglected, and many specimens are seen stuck in a dark corner, covered in dust and bone dry, but still alive – a cast-iron constitution indeed. But give it good compost and regular feeding and you will be rewarded with an impressive show of broad, dark green, healthy foliage. There is a variegated form too: make sure you provide it with good light to make the most of the special effects.

A. elatior 'Variegata'

HOW MUCH LIGHT
Although they cope with shade, aspidistras grow better in good light – but keep out of direct sunlight.

ROOM TEMPERATURE
Tolerates temperatures just above freezing, but happiest at room temperature, 18–24°C (64–75°F).

WHEN TO WATER
Keep the compost just moist and water regularly during the warm summer growing season. Brown spots on leaves are usually a sign of over-watering.

SURVIVAL STRATEGY
Not a fussy plant and easily grown with minimum attention. Keep the leaves clean by wiping them with a damp cloth. Throughout summer provide a balanced liquid feed every 3 weeks.

SIZE
82cm/33in

SITE
Minimalist interior; shady hallway

Asplenium nidus

Bird's-nest fern

Here is a fern that's travelling incognito: it is not immediately recognisable because unlike most ferns the fronds are not divided. Entire shiny pale green fronds unroll from the centre of the rosette and expand, often with wavy edges, to form a "bowl" or "nest" that can be as much as 1m (3ft) across, though it's often much less. Because of its architectural shape and light green colouring it is a good plant for creating a bold, leafy jungle effect. Try it alongside calatheas or aspidistras.

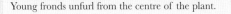
Young fronds unfurl from the centre of the plant.

☼ **HOW MUCH LIGHT**
Direct sun is likely to cause leaves to scorch, so provide dappled shade.

🌡 **ROOM TEMPERATURE**
The winter minimum is 13°C (55°F), but year-round normal temperatures 18–24°C (64–75°F) are better.

💧 **WHEN TO WATER**
Keep the compost well watered through the growing season. During winter periods of no growth keep the compost just moist.

✋ **SURVIVAL STRATEGY**
Young fronds are quite tender and scorch easily in hot sun. Provide a balanced liquid feed every 3 weeks through the growing period but stop during the cooler winter months when no growth occurs. Clean leaves with a damp cloth, but take care: fronds are easily damaged.

📏 **SIZE**
38cm/15in

🏠 **SITE**
Brightly lit kitchen

Dracaena marginata **pp.76–77**

You don't need flowers to say it with plants: many will never flower indoors, but more than compensate with the bold shapes created by their leaves and stems. Choose a plant with a strong architectural shape or a distinctive form and you can give a room a new focal point, or make a dramatic statement with astonishing ease.

Isolepsis cernua **p.105**

Euphorbia trigona **p.82**

Agave attenuata **p.23**

Begonia Rex-cultorum 'Fireworks'

Begonia

There is a begonia to suit almost any situation and taste from bright and colourful flowery hybrids to sophisticated plants with striking foliage; from small plants 2–3cm (1in) high to those well over 1m (3ft). Those known as Rex-cultorum hybrids have some of the most dramatic foliage. Many have large leaves veined or marked with bold patterns of silver, purple, green, or red – and often accessorised with colourful hairy stems. Whether you see them more as flowers or foliage plants, this is a great plant group to explore.

LEAF CUTTINGS Plant a leaf with a 2.5cm (1in) stalk so it rests on the compost surface. A plastic bag helps raise humidity and new plants form in about 2 months.

HOW MUCH LIGHT
Most begonias enjoy bright light away from scorching sunshine.

ROOM TEMPERATURE
Despite their wide variety, begonias all require temperatures ranging around 18–21°C (64–70°F).

WHEN TO WATER
Plants with congested or hairy stems are best watered from below to prevent rotting in their crown.

SURVIVAL STRATEGY
Remove fallen flowers, especially on winter-flowering plants: if left lying on the foliage they will cause rotting. Begonia mildew can be a problem on the leaves of some varieties if the plants are under stress from drought or heat. Remove affected leaves and use a suitable fungicide.

SIZE
33cm/13in

SITE
Living room

Other varieties

B. hatacoa 'Silver' Compact and cool with white flowers adding to the effect. Mildew may be hard to spot. To 30cm (12in) tall.

B. 'Rieger Hybrid' Winter bloomers provide cheerful colour from autumn to spring but are susceptible to mildew. To 40cm (16in).

B. benichoma Striking, mildew-resistant plant with leaves divided into several leaflets atop long upright stems 40–50cm (16–20in) tall.

◁ *B.* 'Red Robin' has ribbed, crinkled, and hairy leaves whose deep red colouring is encouraged by good light. To 25cm (10in).

Billbergia nutans 'Variegata'
Queen's tears

There are several species of bilbergia that may be grown as houseplants, but this is one of the toughest and easiest. The grey-green, arching leaves are 30cm (12in) or so long and develop into a substantial clump. The pendant flowers are an intriguing mix of pink, blue and yellowish green and hang beneath long, showy pink bracts. Provided you keep the plant warm and watered, flowers will be produced almost all year round, but most abundantly during the lighter spring and summer months.

HOW MUCH LIGHT
To ensure good flowering, grow this billbergia in bright light, with direct sunlight for a few hours of the day.

ROOM TEMPERATURE
Tolerates 4°C (39°F) but to ensure regular flowering, keep at 18–24°C (64–75°F) all year.

WHEN TO WATER
Water regularly with soft water, allowing the compost to partially dry out between waterings. It grows almost continuously, so benefits from a fortnightly dose of half-strength balanced liquid feed.

SURVIVAL STRATEGY
An undemanding plant with no special needs beyond good light and regular food and water. The root system is small and quite large plants can be satisfied in small pots, but should they need repotting, do it in spring and use a proprietary bromeliad mix.

SIZE
57cm/23in

SITE
Bright living room

Bougainvillea x *buttiana* hybrids

Paper flower

Left to their own devices, in warm climates these vigorous climbers grow high and wide. Even constrained in pots and with regular cutting back they may reach 1.5m (5ft), as the thorns on their wandering stems latch on to any available support. Strictly speaking the showy parts are papery bracts, which start to reveal their colours (whites, pinks, and reds) in summer. *B. glabra* tends to flower year round, but *B.* x *buttiana* has a rest during winter. Unfortunately many are sold without a variety name, let alone the name of their species: treat them all as if they have a winter rest period and you will not go far wrong.

B. glabra 'Alexandra'

🌞 HOW MUCH LIGHT
Light is absolutely crucial for plants to flower well. Give plenty of direct sun (as much as possible) all year.

🌡 ROOM TEMPERATURE
Enjoy warm summers of 25°C (77°F), but don't stifle them with dry heat. Year round 18–24°C (64–75°F) is fine.

💧 WHEN TO WATER
During the summer growing period, keep well watered, but in winter the compost should be kept only just moist: do not overwater. From late spring to late summer apply a balanced liquid feed every 2 weeks, but every third watering replace that with a high potash tomato type feed.

✋ SURVIVAL STRATEGY
As the bracts show colour, move to out of direct light to prolong the show. Encourage more flowers by bending long new growths around a frame. In autumn prune sideshoots back to 2 or 3 buds of a permanent framework of mature shoots. Remove winter dieback in spring.

📏 SIZE
45cm/18in

🏠 SITE
Conservatory

Brugmansia × *candida*

Angels' trumpets

A very large and dramatic plant, whose old name of *Datura* still lingers. The huge flowers are sweetly scented, particularly in the evening, when in its native South America it attracts pollinating moths. The fragrance is so strong that it can cause intoxication – or so the stories go. Its size makes it unsuitable for small spaces but ideal for conservatories where its large leaves and branching growth add a lush, jungle-like feel. Particularly favoured by whitefly and red spider mite.

HOW MUCH LIGHT
Good light is essential for shapely growth and flowers. Full summer sun is okay if compost is moist.

ROOM TEMPERATURE
Can tolerate 4°C (39°F) if dormant in winter, otherwise 16–25°C (61–77°F) is ideal all year.

WHEN TO WATER
This is a thirsty plant; in summer a mature plant in a warm conservatory will need a daily drenching. Plants kept cool in winter will need far less water, and can be kept just moist until growth commences in spring.

SURVIVAL STRATEGY
In late autumn cut back the stems by a half or more to keep it within bounds. Either keep cool and dryish until spring, or if you have good light keep it warm and watered, and it will soon produce new shoots. Feed regularly in summer with a balanced liquid feed.

SIZE
75cm/30in

SITE
Conservatory; bright living room

Caladium bicolor 'White Christmas'

Angel wings

Angel wings indeed. The papery, almost see-through leaves of the white-patterned varieties have a delicate and ethereal quality achieved by no other plant. Leaves with more green and red are a little less elegant but easier to keep in good condition. Caladiums are not the easiest plants to grow because they need high humidity, high temperatures, and definitely no draughts, but such is their beauty that you might consider using them as temporary plants that are discarded once past their best.

C. bicolor 'Rosebud'

HOW MUCH LIGHT
Bright, filtered or reflected light is ideal; direct sun will scorch the leaves very quickly.

ROOM TEMPERATURE
Requires a warm temperature of around 20–23°C (68–73°F) during the growing period.

WHEN TO WATER
Keep the compost moist when the plant is in active growth. Regular misting will help to maintain high humidity, as will standing it on a tray of wet pebbles. Provide a half-strength balanced liquid feed during summer.

SURVIVAL STRATEGY
These plants grow from corms, dying back and becoming dormant in autumn. Overwinter corms in the dark at around 16°C (61°F) and keep them only just moist. Repot in spring and provide temperatures of 20–22°C (68–72°F) to stimulate growth.

SIZE
65cm/26in

SITE
Bright bathroom

Calathea makoyana

Peacock plant

Although calatheas are not the easiest plants to grow, they're certainly not beyond the skills of an enthusiast. Their appeal rests with the astonishing patterns and veining that many display, and the dark colours of the foliage undersides. Some have lacy see-through leaves, others are robust and boldly decorated. They associate well with one another, but are equally at home mixing with ferns and other plants that enjoy lightly-shaded conditions, and as foils for more flowery plants. With the exception of *C. crocata* their own flowers are not showy and unlikely to be produced inside.

Stunning patterns explain common name.

HOW MUCH LIGHT
Keep out of direct sunshine but provide bright filtered light.

ROOM TEMPERATURE
Ideally maintain year-round levels of around 20°C (68°F) and do not allow them to drop significantly in winter.

WHEN TO WATER
Water regularly with soft water, keeping the compost moist but not wet in summer. Reduce watering in winter when growth is slower. Keep humidity as high as you can: the warmer the temperature, the higher it should be.

SURVIVAL STRATEGY
Protect plants from draughts. Dust spoils the appearance: carefully swash the leaves of an upturned plant in a bowl of lukewarm water to clean it. Hot dry conditions are the enemy, but keep them out of direct sun and moist at the roots and your calatheas will thrive.

SIZE
57cm/23in

SITE
Bathroom; shady living room

Other varieties

C. 'Blue Grass' provides lush fresh-green arching foliage, despite its name, for a shady spot in a humid atmosphere.

C. crocata needs warmth and humidity but is doubly ornamental with flamboyant flowers and dark foliage with purple undersides.

C. majestica copes with low light levels – as its dark foliage testifies. The robust near-black leaves are streaked with white or pink lines.

◁ *C. rufibarba* makes hearty, upright clumps of red-and-green wavy-edged foliage. Look out for red spider mite in dry atmospheres.

Callisia repens

Callisia

This is a busy little plant with small leaves reminiscent of its close relative, *Tradescantia*. It is a creeping plant that you can use either on its own as a trailer – its long stems extend to 50cm (20in) – or to cover the surface beneath other plants in larger pots. It also provides good groundcover for conservatory beds. Small white flowers are produced usually in late summer. *Callisia elegans*, the striped inch plant, has larger foliage with white stripes.

HOW MUCH LIGHT
Provide bright light, ideally with a few hours of early morning or late afternoon sunlight.

ROOM TEMPERATURE
Normal room temperatures 18–24°C (64–75°F) are best, with a winter minimum of 10°C (50°F).

WHEN TO WATER
Keep the compost moist when the plant is in active growth. During the winter resting period allow it to dry out slightly between waterings. Provide a fortnightly dose of half-strength balanced liquid feed.

SURVIVAL STRATEGY
Don't be afraid to trim it back if your plant becomes straggly. Shearing over with scissors stimulates new shoots and freshens up tired-looking plants. Push the bits you cut off into shaded, moist compost and they will soon root.

SIZE
25cm/10in

SITE
East- or west-facing windowsill

Camellia japonica 'Mary Williams'

Camellia

This handsome evergreen woody shrub has glossy dark green, leathery leaves that make the perfect foil for its large, showy flowers. Double or single pink, white, or crimson flowers are produced in late winter and spring. It eventually makes a shrub too large for most homes; plant it in the garden into neutral or acidic soil when it reaches this stage. The flowerbuds are initiated and start to develop between midsummer and early autumn; it is important not to let the plant dry out during this period as this causes the buds to fall off before they have fully opened. Camellias enjoy cool conditions. In warm environments the flowers will be shorter-lived, and, long-term, growth may be straggly.

C. japonica 'Lovelight'

C. japonica 'Jupiter'

HOW MUCH LIGHT
Requires bright light, but keep out of direct sunlight.

ROOM TEMPERATURE
Withstands -5°C (23°F) but the ideal summer range is 16–21°C (61–70°F) and 10–16°C (50–61°F) in winter.

WHEN TO WATER
Use soft water and keep the plant just moist during the winter period. Water well throughout summer. After flowering, provide a balanced liquid feed suitable for lime-hating plants until late summer.

SURVIVAL STRATEGY
Grow camellias in ericaceous (lime-free) compost. Keep the plant within bounds by pruning just after flowering. Look out for black sooty mould on the leaves which indicates the presence of aphids or scale insects (see p.187).

SIZE
90cm/36in

SITE
Cool, well lit hallway

Campanula isophylla

Star-of-Bethlehem

Few trailing plants can boast as much flower power as these blue- or white-flowered campanulas. In spring and summer each stem produces great quantities of flowerbuds which, when fully open, completely hide the foliage. Be warned: high summer temperatures cause flowers to fade and plants to become open and straggly. Once flowering is over, move the plant to cool winter quarters, such as a cold greenhouse or conservatory.

HOW MUCH LIGHT
Keep out of hot, direct sunlight, but provide good light to keep the plant compact.

ROOM TEMPERATURE
Winter lows of 2–10°C (36–50°F) are essential for good flowering. Warm winters will result in fewer flowers.

WHEN TO WATER
Water regularly in summer, keeping compost moist but not wet. Keep it just moist in winter, and water from below to prevent stems and leaves getting too wet and rotting. Provide a fortnightly dose of balanced liquid feed while plants are in flower, but stop when flowering finishes.

SURVIVAL STRATEGY
Pick off spent flowers to stop them rotting on the plant, and encourage more blooms. The congested stems provide ideal conditions for fungal diseases like grey mould if the plant is not kept dry enough, or sufficiently well ventilated in winter. Make sure you clean it up before dormancy.

SIZE
28cm/11in

SITE
East-facing windowsill

Capsicum annuum Conioides Group

Chilli pepper

Ornamental peppers have enduring bright, showy, fleshy fruits which are long and thin or rounded, or somewhere in between. Colours range from cream, yellow, orange, and red to purple, and change as they ripen, creating a harlequin effect. The small white flowers are insignificant. They are annuals, so discard when the fruits wither. You can raise plants from seed; give them warmth and plenty of light.

C. annuum Cerasiforme Group (Cherry pepper)

☼ HOW MUCH LIGHT
Good light with some direct sun is essential – and tricky in winter. Keep it in the brightest spot in the house.

🌡 ROOM TEMPERATURE
Room temperatures of 18–24°C (64–75°F) are sufficient, but fruits last longer in cooler conditions.

💧 WHEN TO WATER
Do not let the plant dry out. Keep the compost moist, but do not allow it to stand in water. Apply a balanced liquid feed every fortnight.

✋ SURVIVAL STRATEGY
If the fruits fall off, check that your plant is getting sufficient light; that it has not been allowed to dry out; that it is out of cold draughts; and that it has not been over-watered.

📏 SIZE
28cm/11in

🏠 SITE
Bright kitchen windowsill

Display ideas | Tricks with texture

Alocasia x *amazonica*, *p.25; Calathea* 'Blue Grass', *pp.40–41*

PLANTS HAVE EVOLVED in response to conditions in the wild: hairy leaves protect against heat, cold, or insect attack; thick, fleshy leaves combat drought. With a spectacular range of textures to choose from, you can use plants as you would fabrics for stunning effects. Soften hard edges with fluffy ferns, cheer stark corners with crinkly leaves, or add shine with glossy green foliage.

Sedum morganianum, **p.150**

Gynura aurantiaca, **p.94**

Selaginella martensii 'Watsoniana', **p.151**

Davillia canariensis, **p.70;** *Asparagus setaceus,* **p.29**

Caryota mitis
Fish-tail palm

A strange-looking palm that almost looks as if it was never quite finished, or as though its leaves have been attacked by nibbling insects. Its odd unpalm-like habit makes it a curiosity and a good talking point, even though some may argue that it is not the most beautiful of plants. But for me, a large specimen has an almost sinister presence that I find attractive. It is not fast-growing so if you want a large one it's better to buy big than to wait for a small one to grow. Use it to provide shade for smaller low-growing foliage plants that enjoy filtered light and share a taste for humidity, such as calatheas and marantas, both of which complement the caryota foliage.

HOW MUCH LIGHT
Provide as much light as possible, but not direct scorching sunlight.

ROOM TEMPERATURE
Requires a minimum of 15°C (59°F) all year, but in temperate zones you can place it outside during summer.

WHEN TO WATER
Keep well watered during summer when light and temperature are good. When growth slows in winter reduce the amount of water, and allow the surface of the compost to dry out before watering.

SURVIVAL STRATEGY
The fact that it is native to Burma and Malaya gives some indication that it likes a warm and humid environment. You can encourage a humid atmosphere by standing it on a tray of moist pebbles (see p.178).

SIZE
1.7m/5½ft

SITE
Airy living room

Ceropegia linearis subsp. *woodii*

Hearts on a string

I like this plant. At a distance all you might notice are the long – up to 2m (6ft) – hanging, wiry stems strung with small, silvery-grey hearts, but close up it is a different story. The surface of each succulent, sea-green heart is patterned with grey and purple, and the underside is a smooth soft pink-purple which just folds around the edge of the leaf to give the textured surface a neat rim. The flowers are small but detailed, and develop into two extraordinarily long needle-like seedpods.

Summer flowers are just 1–2cm (½in) long.

HOW MUCH LIGHT	**WHEN TO WATER**	**SURVIVAL STRATEGY**
Provide plenty of direct light or it will develop spindly stems with poor colouring and spaced out leaves.	Keep the compost moist but not wet when in active growth. In winter give it just enough water to prevent wilting or shrivelling, but beware of over-watering. Give it a half-strength balanced liquid feed every fortnight during the summer months.	This is an undemanding plant. It enjoys direct sunlight and whilst it is best kept moist during the growing season, it will stand the occasional drying out. You can use the small tubers, which develop at intervals along the stems, for propagation.

SIZE
60cm/24in

ROOM TEMPERATURE
Normal room temperature 18–24°C (64–75°F) is sufficient, with a winter minimum of 8°C (46°F).

SITE
Hanging basket; sunny shelf

Chamaedorea elegans

Parlour palm

This is a very common palm much used in conservatories, office receptions, and hotel foyers, which reveals at least one thing: it is tough and easy to grow. It is a leafy plant with several upright stems bearing typical palm leaves that arch over as they get bigger, but it rarely gets taller than 1.5m (5ft). Small yellow flowers may be produced but they are of no real significance. This is an easy-going plant if it is kept out of very dry atmospheres and hot, direct sun, both of which will cause browning of the leaf tips. Keep conservatories well ventilated in summer to prevent stifling temperatures.

HOW MUCH LIGHT
Tolerates shade, but bright, filtered light (not direct, scorching sun) gives you healthier, more compact plants.

ROOM TEMPERATURE
Maintain a winter minimum of 16°C (61°F), otherwise room temperatures of 18–24°C (64–75°F) are sufficient.

WHEN TO WATER
During the summer months water freely, keeping the compost moist at all times. In the cooler winter months it needs less water; allow the top of the compost to dry out before further watering.

SURVIVAL STRATEGY
When the plant is actively growing during summer provide a balanced liquid feed every 2 weeks. Although it tolerates occasional periods of dry air, it prefers a humid atmosphere which you can encourage by standing the plant on a large tray of moist pebbles and regular spraying.

SIZE
66cm/
26½in

SITE
Hallways or stairwells

Chamaerops humilis

Dwarf fan palm

A tough plant in many respects. The stiff and spiny leaves are most attractive as they unfold their compressed pleats, gradually splitting into fan-like fingers. It grows slowly with either a single stem or several short congested stems, all bearing fans that criss-cross and overlap. Over time it can eventually make 1.2m (4ft) and outgrow the average home, but it tolerates several degrees of frost if it's kept dry, and will sit happily outside in full sun during summer.

MANICURING TIPS Unsightly browning leaves may indicate that your plant has been too hot or left too dry. Continually trim off any damaged or brown tips to keep the foliage looking at its best.

HOW MUCH LIGHT
Give it as much light as possible at all times.

ROOM TEMPERATURE
Tolerates frost but 8–10°C (46–50°F) is ideal in winter; prefers 15–24°C (59–75°F) in summer.

WHEN TO WATER
During the summer months water regularly to keep the compost moist. In winter, when growth has stopped, allow the compost to dry out before watering sparingly.

SURVIVAL STRATEGY
This is an easy-going plant that copes well with indoor life if you respect its need for good drainage and an open, loam-based compost, and avoid over-watering it.

SIZE
85cm/34in

SITE
Brightly lit hallway; airy conservatory

Chlorophytum comosum 'Vittatum'

Spider plant

Traditionally one of the most ubiquitous, loved, neglected, and generally abused houseplants, but still one of the best for brightening shady rooms and tolerating such treatment. Be fair to the plant; give it proper care and conditions and it will look twice as good as the specimens found malingering in dark corners. The arching yellow stems, which produce small white flowers and end in cascades of miniature plants, are an added bonus.

HOW MUCH LIGHT
As much as possible in winter, when light levels are low, to maintain good leaf colour. Avoid scorching sun.

ROOM TEMPERATURE
Normal room temperature 18–24°C (64–75°F) is adequate, with a winter minimum of 8°C (46°F).

WHEN TO WATER
Keep compost moist when the plant is active, from spring to autumn. During the winter resting period, reduce watering and allow compost to dry out slightly before watering again. Regular fortnightly doses of balanced liquid feed during the growing period help keep it healthy.

SURVIVAL STRATEGY
Try not to bend the arching leaves: once kinked, they never fully recover and are best cut out low down with scissors. Large fleshy roots pushing out the top of the compost indicate it needs repotting. Brown leaf tips are caused by a dry atmosphere or by being dry at the roots; snip them off.

SIZE
50cm/20in

SITE
Pedestal table; shady living room

Chrysanthemum cultivars

Chrysanthemum

Potted chrysanthemums are ideal for adding short-term cheer and colour to the home. There are plenty to choose from in a wide range of colours to suit any mood or décor, and the plants themselves are undemanding and long flowering. Discard old plants. Young, newly bought plants will have been pinched-out and treated with a dwarfing agent to keep them neat and compact; they become much taller when the effects wear off. If you want to keep old plants then put them in the garden in mild weather, where they can grow tall without worry.

C. 'Zuki'

HOW MUCH LIGHT
Bright light is needed to encourage buds to open and for healthy growth, but keep out of scorching sunlight.

ROOM TEMPERATURE
A cool 13–14°C (55–57°F) is best. Warm conditions cause the flowers to open and fade much more quickly.

WHEN TO WATER
Pot chrysanthemums are often grown several to a pot so that you get more leaf and flower per pot; this means they are particularly thirsty and need regular watering. Soak them from the bottom to avoid getting the crown wet or encouraging the leaves to rot.

SURVIVAL STRATEGY
These are temporary guests so there's no need to feed them. Remove spent flowers to prevent disease and to encourage more buds to open.

SIZE
35cm/14in

SITE
Cool, bright rustic interior

Cissus rhombifolia 'Ellen Danica'

Grape ivy

Strictly speaking this is a climber that uses its tendrils to travel aloft and it is readily trained up a lattice where it will reach a height of 2m (6ft). However, you can just as easily use it without support, allowing it to spill out of its pot and trail downwards. The foliage is softly hairy when young, which gives the new olive-green leaves a silvery gleam; mature foliage turns a glossy dark green. It's an undemanding plant and tolerates a wide range of conditions.

HOW MUCH LIGHT
For sturdy, compact growth choose a brightly lit site out of direct midday sun, which is likely to scorch foliage.

ROOM TEMPERATURE
Grow at normal room temperature 18–24°C (64–75°F) with a winter minimum of 12°C (54°F).

WHEN TO WATER
Water regularly during spring and summer when the plant is actively growing; reduce watering in winter when activity is slower and temperatures are lower. Plants wintering in warm rooms will need more regular watering.

SURVIVAL STRATEGY
You can cut out occasional vigorous shoots at any time, but wait until spring to carry out major cutting back. Regularly tie-in shoots to help keep the plant neat and tidy. Provide monthly doses of balanced liquid feed during the growing season. Do not feed in winter.

SIZE
90cm/36in

SITE
Jungle effect in cool conservatory

× *Citrofortunella microcarpa* syn. *Citrus mitis*
Calamondin orange

This is one of the easier citrus plants to grow. It is something of a charmer, almost guaranteed to add some fruity finishing touches to your home. It's always exciting to grow something that not only looks and smells good, but also offers the chance of edible fruits (they may be a little bitter, but try making your own exclusive jar of marmalade; there is satisfaction to be had from producing a good crop). The scented spring flowers are self-fertile, but give them a dab with a small paintbrush if there are no insects around to shake the pollen up. The plant will benefit from the fresher outdoor environment during summer and, provided it is out of the wind, can be placed outside from early to late summer avoiding the cold nights of spring and early autumn.

KEEPING IN TRIM Cut back sideshoots and growing tips by about one-third to keep the plant compact and bushy. Do this in spring, before flowering, and cut just above a bud.

HOW MUCH LIGHT
Good bright light is vital for good flowering and compact growth.

ROOM TEMPERATURE
Ideal summers of 22–25°C (72–77°F); takes 14°C (57°F) in winter. Provide higher humidity in warm conditions.

WHEN TO WATER
Water regularly during the growing season but during winter, when temperatures are lower, let compost partially dry out before watering. Feed in spring and early summer with a high-nitrogen fertilizer, then continue with a balanced liquid feed until early autumn.

SURVIVAL STRATEGY
A good crop relies on a healthy plant, and that depends on a rich compost, generous feeding, warm temperatures, high humidity, and good light. All citrus are sensitive to cold draughts and respond by losing their leaves. Too much or too little water can also lead to leaf drop.

SIZE
60cm/24in

SITE
Conservatory

Clivia miniata

Kaffir lily

This is a robust evergreen, with beefy strap-like, glossy leaves. The large flowers open in a dense head at the top of a thick stalk, usually towards the end of winter or early spring – there may be as many as 15 warm orange, yellow, or apricot flowers in a single head. Clivias enjoy cramped conditions; don't worry about roots pushing out of the top of the pot, but wait until the plant is almost being forced out of its container by the overcrowded roots before repotting. It is difficult to water pot-bound plants from above, so dunk them in a bucket of water then leave it to drain.

Bursting anthers dust the petals with pollen.

☀ HOW MUCH LIGHT
Give clivias a position in bright light at all times of the year but keep out of midday sun during summer.

🌡 ROOM TEMPERATURE
Prefers cool summers 18°C (64°F) and a low winter resting period at 7–8°C (45–46°F).

💧 WHEN TO WATER
During the growing season water regularly, keeping the compost moist but not wet. In winter keep watering to a minimum. Feed when the plant is actively growing – which will be when the flower is well formed. Stop feeding in late summer.

🤚 SURVIVAL STRATEGY
An easy plant to care for, flowering regularly as long as it is given a rest in early winter. Two months of cooler temperatures around 7°C (45°F) and reduced watering will emulate its natural life cycle and bring it into flower at the right time. Too much warmth shortens the flowering span.

📏 SIZE
68cm/27in

🏠 SITE
Bright living room

Codiaeum variegatum var. *pictum*

Croton

You either love this plant, or hate it. The exotic coloured leaves and stiff habit are not to everyone's taste but whatever you think about it, it certainly cannot be ignored. Apart from their bright red, orange, green, yellow, and occasionally purple colours, the leaves come in a surprising range of shapes too: from long and narrow, to deeply lobed and contorted. If you have the space, grow it large – up to 1m (3ft) – so that its bright colours are balanced by its stature.

C. variegatum var. *pictum* 'Gold Star'

C. variegatum var. *pictum* 'Frank Brown'

HOW MUCH LIGHT
Good light is essential for colours to develop. Likes some direct sun; keep compost moist to prevent scorching.

ROOM TEMPERATURE
Normal room temperature 18–24°C (64–75°F) is sufficient with a winter minimum of 13–14°C (55–57°F).

WHEN TO WATER
Water frequently when temperatures are high during summer, keeping the compost moist but not wet. In winter keep the compost only just moist.

SURVIVAL STRATEGY
Apply a balanced liquid feed fortnightly throughout summer. Keep them small by cutting back in spring, but take care to avoid contact with the white sap which may irritate and inflame your eyes and skin. Do not position these plants in draughts or dry atmospheres.

SIZE
67cm/ 26½in

SITE
Jazz up minimalist interiors

Cordyline australis
Cabbage palm

This is a versatile plant that in temperate climates can be used indoors or out during summer, and brought back inside for winter. It is grown for its fountain of leaves which may be purple-brown, green, or variegated with white, red, or yellow. Youngsters are ideal as centrepieces in small foliage arrangements.
Larger plants will suit a conservatory, where they can withstand high summer temperatures provided you keep them well-watered.

C. fruticosa 'Red Edge' (Good luck tree)

☀ HOW MUCH LIGHT
C. australis does not enjoy shade, so provide as much light as possible, including 2–3 hours of direct sun.

🌡 ROOM TEMPERATURE
A normal range of 18–24°C (64–75°F) is ideal, but plants can survive near-freezing temperatures unharmed.

💧 WHEN TO WATER
Keep moist in summer. If winter temperatures are low, water sparingly, keeping the compost only just moist.

✋ SURVIVAL STRATEGY
This is an easy-going plant that needs minimum attention. Pull off older leaves as they fade and shrivel. Regularly apply a balanced liquid feed during summer to maintain good leaf colour.

📏 SIZE
60cm/24in

🏠 SITE
Conservatory

Crassula ovata syn. *C. argentea*

Money tree

Judging from the number of these plants you see around and the dire neglect many of them suffer yet still survive, this must be one of the toughest houseplants available. It has succulent leaves, often with a thin red edge, and a thick fleshy stem that stores the water that keeps the plant alive when you forget to provide it. Occasionally it produces small white autumn flowers. Fans of feng shui will know that this plant is a symbol denoting wealth and the enjoyment of life —what better reason do you need to grow it? But if you're looking for a low-growing companion for tall succulents, then *C. socialis*, also from South Africa, may do the trick. It makes a spreading mat of fleshy, compact, tufted rosettes barely 10cm (4in) high, and produces white flowers in spring. Give it a winter minumum of 6–7°C (43–45°F) and plenty of light both in winter and summer.

C. socialis

MORE FOR YOUR MONEY Cuttings root easily at any time of year. Plant a 5–10cm (2–4in) section of stem in moist compost, place in a well-lit position out of direct sun, and keep just moist.

☃ HOW MUCH LIGHT
Good light conditions are important especially in winter and a few hours of direct sunlight are beneficial.

🌡 ROOM TEMPERATURE
Happy at 18–24°C (64–75°F). Keep cool in winter when light levels are low to avoid spindly growth.

💧 WHEN TO WATER
During summer allow compost to become partly dry before watering then thoroughly moisten the compost. Do not allow it to stand in a saucer of water. In winter the compost should be kept just moist enough to prevent leaves shrivelling.

🤚 SURVIVAL STRATEGY
Though not quite indestructible this plant tolerates a good deal of neglect. Over-watering is its main enemy. Wipe dust from the leaves occasionally to enjoy their shiny surface. If necessary, pinch out the shoot tips to encourage branching.

📏 SIZE
25cm/10in

🏠 SITE
South-facing windowsill

Display ideas | Effects with repetition

Echeveria 'Duchess of Nuremberg', *p.79*

REGULAR, REPEATED PATTERNS create a sense of calm and reassurance, which need not be at the expense of style. With careful choice of plant, pot, and position, you can make bold statements that are both easy to live with, and to maintain. Strong shapes work best with simple pots, and the greater the number of repeated elements, the more powerful and dramatic the effect.

Zamioculcas zamiifolia, **p.171**

Sansevieria trifasciata var. *laurentii,* **p.147**

Nephrolepis exaltata 'Bostoniensis', **p.120**

Ctenanthe oppenheimiana 'Tricolor'

Never-never plant

The name *Ctenanthe* comes from the Greek "kteis" meaning comb, and "anthos", flower, and refers to the arrangement of the bracts. It also gives a clue as to how to say the name – you pronounce both the "c" and the "t". Despite the complicated label, it is an exciting foliage plant that eventually makes a bushy shape around 1m (3ft) tall. The long, spear-shaped leaves are streaked with cream and green on their upper surfaces with pink suffusing through from the rich red-purple undersides. For the most dramatic effect, position it so you can see the back of the leaves, and their shadows on the wall.

C. burle-marxii

☼ HOW MUCH LIGHT
Provide bright filtered light during summer and as much light as possible in winter.

🌡 ROOM TEMPERATURE
Normal room temperatures 18–24°C (64–75°F) are all it asks for. Takes a dip to 10–12°C (50–54°F) in winter.

💧 WHEN TO WATER
Water freely during summer keeping compost moist, but allow it to dry out in winter; this is especially important if the temperature falls to 10–12°C (50–54°F), as wet compost may cause root rot. If the leaves roll up it indicates that the plant is too dry.

✋ SURVIVAL STRATEGY
A straightforward plant with no extreme requirements. Feed fortnightly when in active growth but avoid feeding during winter. Benefits from extra humidity by spraying or standing it on a tray of damp pebbles, which may help prevent leaves curling in hot conditions.

📏 SIZE
92cm/37in

🏠 SITE
Bright living room

Cuphea ignea 'Variegata'

Cigar flower

A charming, easily grown, small twiggy plant with rich green, variegated leaves. It has a long season – spring to autumn – of narrow tubular red flowers, each tipped with a speck of purple and white "cigar ash": hence the common name. Give it a place in the sun where it can develop its rounded bushy shape and show off a mass of tiny flowers. It can make 60cm (24in) high and wide but is better trimmed back in spring to keep it bushy and within bounds. It looks rather poor after a cold winter but soon develops into a showy, colourful plant in spring.

HOW MUCH LIGHT
Cupheas thrive in bright light and full sun.

ROOM TEMPERATURE
Tolerates near freezing temperatures in winter but extreme cold can cause leaf drop: 8–10°C (46–50°F) is safer.

WHEN TO WATER
Let it dry out slightly between waterings. Plants allowed to become completely dry will lose their leaves but if watered in time will recover and put on a new set of leaves.

SURVIVAL STRATEGY
Feed fortnightly with a balanced liquid feed. In spring it can be cut back by half to maintain a nice full shape and encourage new flowering shoots.

SIZE
33cm/13in

SITE
Sunny windowsill

Cyclamen persicum

Cyclamen

A popular winter-flowering plant, that not only has very showy flowers but also large attractive leaves variously marked with silver. Flowers range from scarlet, through pink, to white, some with streaks and others with coloured edges. Their petals can be twisted or may have frilly edges. Some are scented, and new varieties are produced regularly. Smaller-flowered cultivars have a charm that is sometimes lacking in the large-flowered hybrids; group several of them together in a single pot to create a colourful display. White cyclamen work well with ferns such as *Pteris argyraea* and *Nephrolepis*.

STOP THE ROT Remove spent flowers and yellowing leaves with their stems intact to prevent decaying stalks from rotting the tuber, especially if the stems are densely crowded.

HOW MUCH LIGHT
Plants in bloom should be given full winter light.

ROOM TEMPERATURE
Cyclamen enjoy cool conditions and will flower longer at temperatures around 13–18°C (55–64°F).

WHEN TO WATER
Wait until the leaves just start to wilt before watering. Always water by standing in a deep saucer of water for 10 minutes, then allow to drain.

SURVIVAL STRATEGY
Feed every 3 weeks with a balanced liquid feed. After flowering, discard, or gradually reduce watering until leaves yellow, then stop watering. In late summer or early autumn, clean off and repot tuber. Keep in a bright place with compost just moist until growth starts, then water as normal.

SIZE
35cm/14in

SITE
Bedroom, or any bright room

Cymbidium hybrids
Cymbidium

The easiest orchids to grow in the home. There are many hybrids but often plants are sold with no variety name, relying on their flowers to tempt you into buying them. They vary considerably in height, and flower colours range through pink, white, green, and yellow. All look exotic, and once in flower will last for several weeks.

The labellum (lip) is the most colourful petal.

HOW MUCH LIGHT
Give bright light but avoid scorching sun. Low light levels will discourage flowering.

ROOM TEMPERATURE
Provide a cool winter of 10°C (50°F) for 6–7 weeks, then keep at room temperature (18–24°C/64–75°F).

WHEN TO WATER
These plants resent over-watering, so take care in winter to keep them only just moist. In summer give water when the top of the compost has dried out. When misting the leaves take care to avoid spraying the flowers: they mark easily, and if they remain wet are prone to rotting.

SURVIVAL STRATEGY
Cymbidiums enjoy high humidity; stand on trays of damp pebbles and mist regularly. Use special feeds for plants in flower, and for ones in leafy growth. In mild areas you can move them outside for summer, to open sheltered sites, where they benefit from fresh air and good light levels.

SIZE
65cm/26in

SITE

Bright living room

Cyperus involucratus syn. *C. alternifolius*

Umbrella plant

How many houseplants have you killed
through over-watering? Well, perhaps
you should try the umbrella
plant, which actually likes being
wet at the roots. The common
name has nothing to do with its affinity
for water but everything to do with the
umbrella-like arrangement of the
flowerheads. The tall triangular stems
are topped by a star-like head of what
look like leaves but are in fact bracts
associated with the grass-like
flowers. Grown well it is a very
stylish plant: make the most of its
architectural shape and elegance,
and enjoy the dramatic shadows
cast when it's properly lit.

SPARE UMBRELLAS Shoot tops readily provide
roots and new young plants will quickly form when
they are upturned in a saucer of water. Plant them
up in moist compost when the roots have formed.

HOW MUCH LIGHT
Give it a well lit position with some
direct sunlight, but avoid placing it
in scorching midday sun.

ROOM TEMPERATURE
Normal room temperatures 18–24°C
(64–75°F) are sufficient, with a winter
minimum of 7°C (45°F).

WHEN TO WATER
Make sure the roots are continually
moist. To keep up with the large
amounts of water required by
mature plants in summer, create a
water reservoir by standing the pot
in a shallow saucer so that it always
has a drink on tap (see p.105).

SURVIVAL STRATEGY
Provide a balanced liquid feed in
summer when the plant is actively
growing. Plants in direct light will
need high levels of humidity to
prevent leaf tips from going brown.

SIZE
40cm/16in

SITE
Bright
living room

Cyrtomium falcatum

Japanese holly fern

The robust leathery nature of the leaves gives this fern a very unfernlike character, but hints at its considerable toughness compared to its flimsy indoor cousins. The holly-like foliage is quite unique: use it to add diversity to groups of ctenanthes, davallias, and aspidistras, or amongst orchids, where its pointed leaves will provide a contrast with their rather ordinary foliage.

HOW MUCH LIGHT
Provide bright light but keep out of hot direct sunshine.

ROOM TEMPERATURE
Normal levels of 18–24°C (64–75°F) are sufficient; unconcerned by near-freezing temperatures in winter.

WHEN TO WATER
Keep compost moist throughout the growing season but allow it to dry out slightly between waterings during winter.

SURVIVAL STRATEGY
Very few requirements if you meet its needs for good light and water. Provide a balanced liquid feed every 3 weeks.

SIZE
35cm/14in

SITE
Cool, bright hallway

Dieffenbachia seguine
Dumb cane

Bold markings and fresh green colouring make this
lively plant guaranteed to brighten your home. A word
of warning: the sap is toxic and can
cause swelling and even loss of speech if
you get it in your mouth – hence the
common name. There are many varieties
all with different markings but equally easy
to care for, provided the
atmosphere is not too dry.
Move them closer to windows
in winter so they get as much
light as possible
during shorter,
darker days.

D. seguine 'Saturn'

☁ HOW MUCH LIGHT
Bright filtered light helps maintain
leaf colour.

🌡 ROOM TEMPERATURE
Winter minimum is 16°C (61°F).
Avoid hot summer temperatures if
you cannot provide high humidity.

💧 WHEN TO WATER
Keep compost moist throughout
the growing season. Low winter
temperatures will check growth
and watering can then be reduced:
allow the plant to partly dry out
before watering.

✋ SURVIVAL STRATEGY
Brown leaf tips may be a sign of
insufficient water, or indicate that the
atmosphere is too dry. Stand it on a
tray of damp pebbles (see p.178).
Don't forget the sap is toxic, so take
care how you handle it, particularly
when removing old leaves.

📏 SIZE
50cm/20in

🏠 SITE
Bright
hallway

Dizygotheca elegantissima syn. *Schefflera elegantissima*

False aralia

This plant creates a busy effect and can be used as a foil for larger leaved plants. The long narrow leaves are a very dark green, which also makes it good to contrast with the lighter coloured foliage of epipremnum or variegated figs (*Ficus*). On its own it makes a tall stately specimen and against a pale plain backdrop the effect of its silhouette can be extremely striking.

HOW MUCH LIGHT
Bright light will keep the growth compact and the leaves a good dark colour. Keep out of hot direct sun.

ROOM TEMPERATURE
Normal room temperature 18–24°C (64–75°F) is sufficient, with a winter minimum of 13°C (55°F).

WHEN TO WATER
This plant is much more tolerant of drying out than it is of over-watering. Allow compost to dry out slightly between waterings, and water sparingly in winter. Misting is beneficial, but use soft water to avoid leaving unsightly white lime marks on the dark foliage.

SURVIVAL STRATEGY
Dizygothecas normally have an upright habit; pinching out the tips will encourage bushier growth.

SIZE
33cm/13in

SITE
Minimalist interiors

Caladium bicolor hybrids, **p.39**

GROUP ARRANGEMENTS look attractive, and can be functional too: a few tall plants can make a flexible living partition to screen off part of a room. Plants also benefit from the higher levels of humidity generated when they are grown close together. And by moving plants with similar needs into a single pot, you can prolong the interest of a flowering display after the blooms have gone.

Philodendron erubescens, **pp.134–135;** *Ficus deltoidea,* **pp.86–87;** *Philodendron* 'Cobra'; *Epipremnum aureum* 'Marble Queen', **p.80**

Calathea zebrina, C. picturata, C. louisae, **pp.40–41;** *Dracaena,* **p.76–77**　　*Exacum,* **p.83;** *Pilea,* **p.137;** *Hypoestes,* **p.101;** *Saintpaulia,* **p.146**

Dracaena marginata

Madagascar dragon tree

Dracaenas are a useful and reliable group of architectural foliage plants. The tufts of narrow leaves are perched elegantly at the top of spindly trunks and the taller they get, the more elegant they become. Lower leaves are shed as the shoot grows higher. Large specimens are best displayed against a plain background to emphasise their striking shape. *D. fragrans* and its varieties are more substantial but less refined: the broader leaves may have greater presence but their style of presentation is heavy handed, with usually a single head on a much stockier trunk.

CALLING CARDS Adult vine weevils leave telltale notches in leaf edges. They are nocturnal, so pick them off at night.

HOW MUCH LIGHT
Enjoys bright conditions. D. fragrans also tolerates semi-shaded positions without losing its variegation.

ROOM TEMPERATURE
Normal room temperature 18–24°C (64–75°F) is sufficient. Avoid winter dips below 14–15°C (57–59°F).

WHEN TO WATER
Keep the compost moist during the growing season but in winter allow compost to dry out partly, before watering sparingly.

SURVIVAL STRATEGY
Cutting the top off single stemmed plants of D. marginata will cause side branches to shoot. Do this in late spring. Gently pull off spent lower leaves to keep the plant tidy.

SIZE
90cm/36in

SITE
Living room

Other varieties

D fragrans Deremensis Group 'Yellow Stripe'
The margins broaden as the arching leaves
expand to their full length of 40cm (16in).

D. marginata 'Tricolor' An "improved" take
on the species with stripes in 3 colours on
arching leaves 30–60cm (12–24in) long.

D. fragrans Broad, plain green arching leaves
up to 80cm (32in) long emerge from a stout
trunk. If you get flowers, they are fragrant.

◁ *D. fragrans* Deremensis Group 'Lemon
and Lime' Tough foliage, arching out to
60cm (24in), for shady or well lit conditions.

Epipremnum aureum 'Marble Queen'

Devil's ivy

A versatile plant that climbs or trails depending on whether or not you give it support. Its stems can reach 2m (6ft) or more, but you can wind them round on themselves to keep the plant compact or pinch out the tips to encourage branching. A moss pole offers good support if you want it to climb. The leathery leaves are a strong shape and have a healthy shine – keep them clean to appreciate it. Variegated forms need plenty of light for the markings to be at their best. Varieties with completely yellow leaves are also available.

HOW MUCH LIGHT
Tolerates quite a shady position but responds to good light conditions with more vigorous growth.

ROOM TEMPERATURE
Normal room temperatures 18–24°C (64–75°F) with a winter minimum of around 14°C (57°F).

WHEN TO WATER
Water regularly during spring and summer but let the plant dry out slightly between waterings. Reduce watering in winter when the plant is less active. Provide a foliage feed in summer when growth is active.

SURVIVAL STRATEGY
If you want it to, this plant will cover a large area of wall – just give it the support of wires or a lattice. Tying-in stems to the support, rather than tucking them through or behind the framework, will make life easier if you need to repot or replace the plant at a later date.

SIZE
50cm/20in

SITE
Hanging basket

Euphorbia pulcherrima 'Pepride™ Marble'

Poinsettia

The red-flowered form (strictly, red bracts) has become a traditional plant for Christmas, despite being a relatively recent introduction and a native of Mexico. Cheer the house in winter by combining them with berried holly, or tone down their vibrant reds by mixing with cooler white varieties; the subtle greenish-whites are well worth a try. To keep after Christmas, wait until bracts begin to fade, then cut stems back to 10cm (4in). Keep warm but barely moist during late winter and early spring. In April give the plant a good soak to bring it into growth. When growing well, repot in the same pot with fresh compost.

E. pulcherrima

'Lilo White'

'Regina'

'Lilo'

HOW MUCH LIGHT
Enjoys bright filtered light at all stages of growth. Scorching sunshine will cause damage.

ROOM TEMPERATURE
Comfortable room temperatures of 18–24°C (64–75°F) are ideal. Avoid placing in cold draughts.

WHEN TO WATER
Wait until the leaves just show signs of wilting then give the compost a good soak. Do not allow the plant stand in water. If you intend to discard it after blooming, no feeding is necessary, otherwise provide a half-strength balanced liquid feed every fortnight.

SURVIVAL STRATEGY
You'll need patience to keep a plant from year to year; flowers and bracts are only initiated when nights last 12 hours or more. For more flowers, provide 14 hours of unbroken, total darkness every day for at least 8 weeks from mid autumn – cover it with a bin liner or plastic bucket.

SIZE
45cm/18in

SITE
Bright living room

Euphorbia tirucalli

Pencil cactus

There are very few plants like this succulent euphorbia and it is difficult to believe that it's a close relative of the poinsettia – but it is. New growth carries small, narrow leaves for a short time, but these eventually fall off leaving a skeletal arrangement of bare, fleshy branches: ideal if you're looking for something to complement minimalist décor. It has evolved into such a shape to survive hot and dry conditions – which makes it perfect for a large south-facing window or conservatory. I would encourage you to give this plant some space and allow it to grow into a very big and impressive specimen.

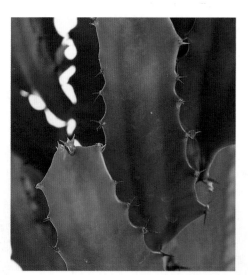

E. trigona

☼ HOW MUCH LIGHT
As much light as possible all year. Move to the sunniest spot during winter when light levels are low.

🌡 ROOM TEMPERATURE
Normal temperature is sufficient but it tolerates higher. Accepts a winter minimum of 10–11°C (50–52°F).

💧 WHEN TO WATER
During summer water sparingly allowing the compost to partly dry out between waterings. In winter give it just enough water to prevent the compost drying out completely.

✋ SURVIVAL STRATEGY
Apply a monthly balanced liquid feed during summer. Beware of bruised or broken branches. These exude a white sap that can cause severe skin irritation in some people, particularly under strong sunlight.

📏 SIZE
80cm/32in

🏠 SITE
Conservatory: south-facing window

Exacum affine
Persian violet

This is a cheerful little plant that produces masses of tiny, fragrant blue, white, or pink flowers over a period of several months. It is a short-lived perennial plant that is usually treated as an annual and discarded when it eventually stops flowering. Young plants are neat and compact but open up with age. You can raise them yourself from seed sown in spring – prick out and pot them on – but if you are weighing the effort and time this involves against buying a ready-grown one, then the shop-bought plant wins hands down.

HOW MUCH LIGHT
Give bright light, but not direct midday sunlight.

ROOM TEMPERATURE
Room temperature is adequate with a minimum of 11°C (52°F) if you want to keep your plant over winter.

WHEN TO WATER
Keep the compost moist throughout the growing season. Provide a balanced liquid feed every fortnight.

SURVIVAL STRATEGY
Regular deadheading prolongs the flowering period. The higher the temperature the greater the need for humidity. Stand on a tray of moist pebbles if your air is dry (see p.178).

SIZE
22cm/9in

SITE
Bright table top display

Fatsia japonica

Japanese aralia

A common but useful plant, with the advantage that it tolerates the cool conditions found by front doors and in unheated conservatories in winter. The leaves are large and glossy and although mature plants may produce heads of white flowers, the majority of plants grown indoors never do. A compact version, *F. japonica* 'Moseri', is also worth a try.

F. japonica 'Variegata'

☁ HOW MUCH LIGHT
Grow in bright light for compact growth and dark green leaves.

🌡 ROOM TEMPERATURE
Keep cool: temperatures as low as 2–3°C (36–37°F) in winter, will result in compact healthy-looking plants.

💧 WHEN TO WATER
Water regularly in summer but reduce watering during winter. Wilting leaves will soon tell you that it is ready for a drink. Regular applications of foliage plant feed will keep the plant's leaves dark green.

✋ SURVIVAL STRATEGY
Clean the leaves with a damp cloth. Do not be afraid to cut back stems of plants that get too tall. Prune them in spring and new sideshoots will soon form to make a bushier plant. Be aware that combinations of high temperatures and low light levels lead to straggly, drawn growth.

📏 SIZE
56cm/22in

🏠 SITE
Bright hallway

Ferocactus latispinus

Devil's tongue

There is not much sitting on the fence when it comes to the barrel cactus: you either love their dumpy leafless growth, furrowed stems, and array of tough, curled, and often colourful spines, or you look at them and wonder what all the fuss is about. With *F. latispinus* the devil is definitely in the detail. Each bristly set is made up of ten or twelve small whitish spines and four big, red, extremely tough ones, of which the lowest, and largest, curls back. The whole plant is an untouchable delight of texture, shape, and subtle colour with – if you are lucky and conditions are ideal – a purple, red, or yellow flower or two.

Prominent curved bristles resemble fish hooks.

 HOW MUCH LIGHT
Light is the all important factor. Provide as much direct sunlight as possible, even in winter.

ROOM TEMPERATURE
Normal to high room temperatures are ideal, combined with good light. Winter minimum is 7°C (45°F).

WHEN TO WATER
Water regularly in summer but do not keep the compost permanently wet and allow it to dry out between waterings. Keep dry during winter. Benefits from a monthly balanced liquid feed during the warm summer period.

SURVIVAL STRATEGY
Place it outdoors once the danger of frost has passed if it means it will get more light. Use a paintbrush to keep the plant clean, or blow off dust with a drinking straw or a vacuum cleaner adjusted to low suck.

SIZE
20cm/8in

 SITE
South-facing windowsill

Ficus elastica
India rubber fig

The fig family provides some excellent plants for the home. In their native habitat many make huge trees but in the confines of a pot they stay small and manageable – although they make impressive specimens if you have the space and want them big. Rubber plant (*F. elastica*) and weeping fig (*F. benjamina*) are well known and reliable favourites, and rightly so: they are particularly good at removing harmful pollutants from the air. *F. benjamina* is naturally bushy, but to get *F. elastica* to branch out you need to cut off the growing point when it is small. Do not worry about the white sap that flows out of the cut, it will stop eventually and causes the plant no harm.

F. elastica 'Belgica'

HOW MUCH LIGHT
Often consigned to shady conditions, but figs are healthier in good light, especially the variegated forms.

ROOM TEMPERATURE
All are satisfied with normal room tempertaure (18–24°C (64–75°F).

WHEN TO WATER
Figs with leathery leaves tolerate being dry better than being too wet. Let the compost become partially dry before watering. Over-watering causes leaf drop. Ficus pumila has thiner leaves and should not be allowed to dry out.

SURVIVAL STRATEGY
Figs adapt well to conditions in the home and are among the easiest plants to grow indoors. Feed fortnightly when actively growing. Wipe leaves clean with a damp cloth.

SIZE
60cm/24in

SITE
Home office; living room

Other varieties

F. sagittata is a small bushy trailing plant with narrow fresh green leaves and a spreading habit, which grows just 15–20cm (6–8in) tall.

F. benjamina 'Starlight' is a form of the bushy weeping fig, which can top 2m (6ft). Good light is essential to maintain the variegation.

F. binnendijkii 'Alii' is upright with narrow leaves around 20cm (8in) long. It prefers bright light, and grows over 2m (6ft) tall.

◁ *F. deltoidea* (Mistletoe fig) Naturally bushy, this is the only ornamental fig likely to bear "figs". Alas they are inedible. To 2m (6ft).

Fittonia verschaffeltii

Painted net leaf

This may be a small plant but it's one with considerable charm. Its oval leaves are prettily veined in white or pink depending on the variety. The low-growing creeper spreads gradually, but the shoots root as they go, which means it is easy to propagate. A wide, shallow pot of several plants makes a more appealing display than a single lone fittonia. It is a plant of the South American rainforests and therefore requires high humidity and warm temperatures; try it in a bottle garden, or a terrarium.

HOW MUCH LIGHT
Give bright filtered light but keep it out of direct sunlight.

ROOM TEMPERATURE
Try to maintain a year-round temperature of 18°C (64°F), along with good humidity.

WHEN TO WATER
Beware of over-watering fittonias, particularly in winter, as the stems may rot. In summer, keep the compost moist but not wet.

SURVIVAL STRATEGY
Warmth and high humidity are essential. Provide a half-strength balanced liquid feed during the summer months when the plant is in full growth.

SIZE
20cm/8in

SITE
Bathroom

Gardenia augusta
Cape jasmine

Gardenias are well-known for their flowers and dark, leathery, evergreen foliage. Growing one is not difficult; getting it to flower again is a different matter. Stable temperatures and humidity are crucial. Sudden temperature changes, draughts, or fluctuating humidity may cause bud drop, as can changing the angle of its light source. Given the fussy demands, you may decide to enjoy it while the flowers last, then buy another next year.

Pure white flowers are deliciously scented.

HOW MUCH LIGHT
Position in good bright light but out of direct scorching sun.

ROOM TEMPERATURE
To encourage flowers, provide high humidity and 18–21°C (64–70°F) by day and 16–17°C (61–63°F) at night.

WHEN TO WATER
Use soft water to prevent the leaves yellowing. Keep the compost moist but not wet during summer: reduce watering during the darker winter months. In summer give it a liquid feed specifically formulated for lime-hating plants.

SURVIVAL STRATEGY
Grow in a lime-free compost, and provide stable temperatures and humidity. For flowers, ensure night temperatures fall below 18°C (64°F); day temperatures must be no higher than 22°C (72°F). Avoid draughts, or moving its position so that it is at a different angle to its light source.

SIZE
35cm/14in

SITE
Living room

Graptopetalum bellum

Graptopetalum

This small tightly packed succulent punches way above its weight when it comes to flowering. The fleshy leaves form a tight, mounded rosette that rarely gets above a few centimetres high and just one or two more across, but the flowers are large, bright and eye-catching. As long as the plant has plenty of light the deep pink-red flowers are freely produced, and once in flower the show lasts for several weeks. When not in flower it can look a little lost if grown on its own, so put several together in a wide shallow pot.

Star-shaped flowers

HOW MUCH LIGHT
Provide as much direct sunlight as possible throughout the year.

ROOM TEMPERATURE
Normal temperatures are sufficient. Cool winters will help to keep it compact when light levels are low.

WHEN TO WATER
From spring to early autumn when the plant is actively growing water regularly but let the compost dry out slightly between waterings. In winter give just enough water to prevent the compost drying out completely.

SURVIVAL STRATEGY
Over-watering, particularly during winter, causes root rot. Check to see that the plant is not standing in water inside its cachepot.

SIZE
23cm/9in

SITE
South-facing window

Grevillea robusta

Silky oak

If you like plants that get a move on and you do not mind them on the large size then this is the one for you. In its native Australia it reaches 15m (50ft) or more but it can certainly be contained in the home for a few years before it outgrows its space. With its fine leaves and graceful habit, it is a very attractive foliage plant, particularly effective when grown amongst larger, heavier-leaved plants such as philodendron or the Swiss cheese plant (*Monstera*). Be prepared to start again after a few years with a new smaller plant.

HOW MUCH LIGHT
Provide bright light, even full sun. Good light is essential, so move it to the sunniest spot in winter.

ROOM TEMPERATURE
Ordinary room temperature 18–24°C (64–75°F) is sufficient, with a winter minimum of around 5°C (41°F).

WHEN TO WATER
Use soft water. When the plant is actively growing, water regularly keeping compost moist but not wet. When growth is slower in winter allow compost to dry out slightly before watering.

SURVIVAL STRATEGY
Use an ericaceous (lime-free) compost when potting up this fast-growing plant. Provide a liquid feed formulated for lime-hating plants every fortnight throughout the summer growing season.

SIZE
95cm/38in

SITE
Conservatory

Gynura aurantiaca

Purple velvet plant

This looks like the sort of plant you might come across if
you were to land on an alien planet. The combination of its
covering of purple hairs, the toothed and curled leaves, and
its smelly orange winter flowers (pinch them off if you
cannot bear their aroma) give it an outrageous character
that I find irresistible. It starts off quite upright, but
eventually grows sideways and trails out of the pot.

Purple hairs on leaves provide the velvety texture.

☁ HOW MUCH LIGHT
For the best colour grow this plant in
good, bright light.

🌡 ROOM TEMPERATURE
Normal temperatures are sufficient
with moderate humidity. The winter
minimum is 12–13°C (54–55°F).

☂ WHEN TO WATER
Avoid getting water on the leaves.
Keep the compost just moist during
summer but reduce watering in
winter when temperatures drop.

✋ SURVIVAL STRATEGY
An easy-to-please plant. It will root
from pieces of broken-off stem
placed in water. You can keep plants
compact by pinching out stems, but
its trailing habit accounts for a big
part of its character, so not too much
pruning please.

⌀ SIZE
20cm/8in

🏠 SITE
East- or
west-facing
window

Hedera helix 'Light Fingers'

Common ivy

Ivies offer an almost limitless choice of leaf shapes and sizes and although colour is limited to greens, yellows, and whites, there's going to be at least one to suit your taste. There are ivies that climb, ivies that trail, and ivies that make bushy shrubs; all thrive in bathroom, bedroom or living room as long as they get some light and are watered occasionally. More lavish treatment results in healthier, robust plants.

'White Wonder'   'Pink 'n' Curly'

'Gilded Hawke'   'Kolibri'

 **HOW MUCH LIGHT**
Variegated forms benefit from bright light; plain varieties tolerate shade but are more compact in good light.

ROOM TEMPERATURE
Too much heat results in straggly, drawn growth. Grow in conditions as cool as possible all year round.

WHEN TO WATER
Keep moist in summer and do not allow plants to dry out during winter as their leaves will shrivel up.

SURVIVAL STRATEGY
These are very easy plants to grow. A major plus is that they are both shade- and cold-tolerant, making them ideal for a draughty hallway or an unheated conservatory.

SIZE
29cm/11in

 SITE
Bedroom; bathroom

Hemigraphis 'Exotica'

Purple waffle plant

A low-growing compact evergreen with rounded, crinkly leaves that are deeply corrugated and puckered. The foliage is flushed with dark red and purple, almost to the point of appearing black. It bears white flowers from spring to summer which stand out well against the dark leaves. It is not the showiest plant but it has understated class and is great as groundcover for plants in large pots. Alternatively, use a few individuals as a unifying feature in group displays. With its compact habit, this is a useful plant for a narrow windowsill or as a filler amongst larger plants.

HOW MUCH LIGHT
Bright light encourages good leaf colour and flowering. Keep out of scorching sun.

ROOM TEMPERATURE
Normal room temperature 18–24°C (64–75°F). Do not allow it to fall below 12–13°C (54–55°F) in winter.

WHEN TO WATER
Water regularly during the summer months when the plant is in active growth. Reduce watering in winter but do not allow it to become dry.

SURVIVAL STRATEGY
Hemigraphis enjoys the humidity of a micro-environment created by surrounding plants. The higher the temperature, the greater the need for humidity.

SIZE
30cm/12in

SITE
Bright windowsill

Hibiscus rosa-sinensis 'Athene'

Rose of China

A very leafy and bushy plant with flamboyant flowers in a wide range of colours – red, white, orange, pink, and yellow. The main flowering season is during summer but given warm temperatures and good light, flowers may appear on and off all year round. Even when out of flower the branching habit and dark green leaves make an attractive addition to the general greenery in the house. Give it pride of place, cherish it, and you will be well rewarded.

H. rosa-sinensis

☼ HOW MUCH LIGHT
Plenty of bright light but not midday summer sun. In winter give it full sun, but keep it moist at the roots.

🌡 ROOM TEMPERATURE
Normal temperature is sufficient. Stifling conservatory heat without humidity causes flowers to fade fast.

✋ WHEN TO WATER
Large plants will need regular watering during summer: keep the compost moist. In winter reduce watering and allow the compost to dry out slightly before the next watering.

✋ SURVIVAL STRATEGY
Given a large pot and enough space specimens can grow to 2m (6ft) or more, but if you prune back hard in spring you can keep them within bounds. This does not affect flowering. A high potash feed during early summer encourages flowering.

SIZE
50cm/20in

🏠 SITE
Airy conservatory

Hippeastrum cultivars
Amaryllis

Hippeastrums manage to combine, on the same plant, some of the most flamboyant flowers with some of the plainest and least interesting leaves. That said, you can certainly overlook its foliage failings when it is in full, overwhelming bloom. Colours of the large trumpet flowers can be anything from blood red to pure white or pale green and each head can carry as many as five blooms. Emphasize their architectural qualities and divert attention from the gaunt foliage by growing in a regimental line in a long trough or as repeated patterns in a row of identical pots.

Open trumpets reveal pollen-laden anthers.

HOW MUCH LIGHT
When in leaf, provide plenty of light including some direct sun. Too little, and plants are unlikely to flower.

ROOM TEMPERATURE
Will flower at normal temperatures 18–24°C (64–75°F); keep cool when in bloom to prolong the display.

WHEN TO WATER
Dry bulbs should be potted up and kept just moist until roots develop and start to take up water; thereafter keep compost moist at all times in active growth. In late summer stop watering, let the bulb dry off and leaves wither. Start watering again in autumn to bring it into growth.

SURVIVAL STRATEGY
Getting flowers second time around takes a little care. After flowering, when leaves appear, feed and water regularly and give good light. Allow for a dormant period in late summer, and in autumn bring it back into growth. When actively growing, repot into fresh compost in the same pot.

SIZE
74cm/29in

SITE
Minimalist interior

Howea belmoreana

Sentry palm

An upright and potentially large palm (2m/6ft plus) with the major advantage that it is tough and tolerates less-than-ideal conditions. It grows in low humidity and will tolerate low light levels – but do not expect it to grow in the dark. Although a howea will endure difficult conditions, when given good light with reasonable humidity it will respond with greater vigour and develop into a healthier and more handsome plant. Elegant, deeply cut, arching fronds on stiff upright stems make it ideal for standing at the back of a group of shorter plants, or use it to throw shapely shadows across plain walls.

HOW MUCH LIGHT
Enjoys well-lit sites but copes with medium light. Move nearer windows to maximise low winter light levels.

ROOM TEMPERATURE
Give a winter minimum of 13–14°C (55–57°F), otherwise keep at room temperature 18–24°C (64–75°F).

WHEN TO WATER
Keep compost moist during the growing season. Reduce watering in winter and give just enough to prevent the compost drying out completely. Apply a balanced liquid feed fortnightly in the growing season; stop feeding in winter.

SURVIVAL STRATEGY
This is an amenable plant that needs little extra attention as long as it is fed and watered. Wipe dust off the leaves with a damp cloth or sponge; it is a time consuming but – when you see the results – satisfying job.

SIZE
85cm/34in

SITE
Bright south-facing living room

Hoya lanceolata subsp. *bella*

Wax flower

There are several hoya species available to the indoor gardener but of them all this is the most manageable and compact. Often sold as just *Hoya bella* this succulent trailing plant with diamond-shaped leaves has clusters of sweetly scented white flowers each with a purple centre. In summer you'll find between eight and ten quite large flowers at the end of each branch. A hanging basket will place the flowers at just the right height for you to appreciate their strong fragrance.

Clusters of summer flowers are sweetly scented.

☼ HOW MUCH LIGHT
To ensure good flowering give plenty of light. This can be direct sunlight, but not scorching midday sun.

🌡 ROOM TEMPERATURE
Normal room temperature 18–24°C (64–75°F) is suitable all year.

💧 WHEN TO WATER
Water regularly in summer. Reduce watering during winter when the plant is not growing. Apply a half-strength balanced liquid feed every fortnight.

🖐 SURVIVAL STRATEGY
Grow in an open compost, like that used for orchids. Related Hoya carnosa will make 4–5m (12–15ft) in height but can be looped in a circle or wrapped around a frame to keep it within bounds.

SIZE
55cm/22in

🏠 SITE
Well lit table top

Hypoestes phyllostachya 'Ruby'

Polka dot plant

If you have ever hastily painted your walls using a roller before covering all your furniture you will have some idea of the speckled nature of this plant. Each heart-shaped leaf of this small shrubby plant is covered in pink dots. Varieties with larger markings and some with purple, white, or red splashes on the leaves are available. They are fun plants and a collection of all the varieties in a single pot or grouped together provides useful colour all year round.

'Rose'

'White'

HOW MUCH LIGHT
For the best colours keep in bright light but out of hot direct summer sun. Tolerates direct sun in winter.

ROOM TEMPERATURE
Keep warm. A year round constant of 18°C (64°F) is ideal. Long periods below 11°C (52°F) cause leaf drop.

WHEN TO WATER
Give ample water during summer but allow the compost surface to dry between waterings. Water less in winter, and beware of over-watering. It will enjoy a humid atmosphere.

SURVIVAL STRATEGY
The plant has a tendency to become leggy and open over time so during spring or summer trim back and pinch out the growing tips to encourage bushiness. Provide a balanced liquid feed in summer; stop feeding in the winter months.

SIZE
20cm/8in

SITE
Bathroom; living room

Display ideas | Natural air fresheners

Ficus benjamina, **pp.86–87**

PLANTS PROVIDE THE OXYGEN WE BREATHE: no plants, no life. Many also prove their worth as great filters of volatile household pollutants, including formaldehyde, ammonia, and benzene, given off by upholstery, paints, and domestic motors. Choose plants that absorb these chemicals for bedrooms, living rooms, and offices, to make your indoor environment fresher and safer.

Chlorophytum comosum 'Vittatum', **p.52**

Calathea makoyana, **pp.40–41**

Spathiphyllum wallisii, **p.160**

Impatiens hybrids
Busy Lizzie

Though most commonly used for summer bedding, busy Lizzies make exceptionally colourful and easy houseplants. Flowering starts in early summer and continues through until late autumn but if light and temperature conditions are right it produces flowers right through winter too. Any of those offered as bedding plants can be potted up for indoor use to make profusely flowering bushy plants for a cool windowsill or lightly shaded interior position. Look out for those raised from pure bred F1 Hybrid seed, which produce large, vigorous, healthy plants. Pinch out the growing tips for a bushier effect.

F1 Hybrid 'White'

F1 Hybrid 'Red'

HOW MUCH LIGHT
Provide bright light, but keep out of the direct heat of the midday sun.

ROOM TEMPERATURE
Enjoys cool conditions, but room temperature will do, with a winter minimum of 13–14°C (55–57°F).

WHEN TO WATER
Keep plants moist but not wet throughout the growing season, and water sparingly during winter.

SURVIVAL STRATEGY
Deadhead regularly. Plants may be discarded at the end of summer, or kept through winter. They require good light and warmth to continue flowering in winter. Cut back overwintered plants in spring. Old plants may be replaced with 3–4cm (1½in) shoot tips, rooted in water.

SIZE
20cm/8in

SITE
Lightly shaded living room

Isolepis cernua

Slender club-rush

A plant with no bright flowers and no colourful leaves but
plenty of character. Isolepis grows naturally at the water's edge,
but it's a fascinating plant to have inside. It makes a clump of
spiky grass-like foliage carrying tiny flowers which
appear to be just stuck on the side of the leaf –
and is as near as you're going to get to
a natural fibre optic bush. It is
the perfect addition to a
contemporary-styled
interior in which
shape, texture,
and uniformity
are all.

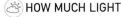

WET FEET Moisture-loving plants grow naturally
in damp, peaty places, so keep the compost moist
at all times. You can create the conditions they
prefer by standing the pot in a reservoir of water.

HOW MUCH LIGHT
Full, bright light is essential for
strong compact growth.

ROOM TEMPERATURE
A tough plant that will cope with cool
conditions below 16°C (61°F) better
than high temperatures.

WHEN TO WATER
This is a moisture-loving plant, so
keep the compost moist at all times,
and use soft water.

SURVIVAL STRATEGY
Give it plenty of ventilation and avoid
high temperatures, and you have a
largely trouble-free houseguest.

SIZE
25cm/10in

SITE
Minimalist
interior

Kalanchoe pumila
Kalanchoe

There is a startling range of kalanchoes, with plenty of shapes, styles, and colours to choose from. *K. pumila* has neat grey-green serrated leaves perfectly complemented by its purple-pink flowers, but the succulent foliage of *K. tomentosa* offers something completely different, with its silver hairs tinted brown at the leaf edges. Such variety means kalanchoes will appeal to anyone of a botanical bent wanting to start a collection. Despite appearances, their cultural needs are not so wildly different that you cannot grow them all in the same conditions.

Pink, urn-shaped flowers appear in spring.

☼ HOW MUCH LIGHT
Plenty of good light: all stand some direct sunlight – the greyer or hairier they are, the more sun they need.

🌡 ROOM TEMPERATURE
Normal room temperature; tolerate cooler winter levels as long they do not drop much below 10°C (50°F).

💧 WHEN TO WATER
Kalanchoes are best kept on the dry side and watered from the bottom. Allow the compost to partly dry out between waterings, and water sparingly in winter. K. blossfeldiana in particular will suffer when over-watered – getting the heart of the plant wet will cause rot.

✋ SURVIVAL STRATEGY
Avoid over-watering. Remove spent flowers on K. blossfeldiana to prevent flowerheads falling into the heart of the plant and rotting. Feed K. blossfeldiana every fortnight with a balanced liquid feed. Other kalanchoes may be fed monthly.

📏 SIZE
45cm/18in

🏠 SITE
Bathroom

Other varieties

K. blossfeldiana 'Calandiva' (Flaming Katy)
The tight clusters of sophisticated rosebud
flowers on this plant grow to 30cm (12in).

K. mangini hybrids have the largest blooms,
and a long flowering season. Their open
branching stems reach 25–30cm (10–12in).

K. blossfeldiana (Flaming Katy) hybrids come
in bright reds and pastels. Fowers last up to
12 weeks, but plants may not bloom again.

◁ *K. tomentosa* is an irresistible tactile delight.
The brown edge fades as leaves mature but is
prolonged by full sun. Grows to 1m (3ft).

Lantana camara
Lantana

This is both a popular tender perennial for patio plantings in temperate gardens, and one of the worst weeds of commercial plantations in sub-tropical parts of the world. It is also a very attractive and long-flowering houseplant. The individual flowers in each cluster change colour as they mature, creating a rainbow effect. Colours range from orange-white, to red, and pink. Shiny dark blue berries – not to be eaten – follow the flowers.

L. camara 'Snow White'

☼ HOW MUCH LIGHT
Bright light is essential: give it several hours of direct sun a day and move to the lightest place for winter.

🌡 ROOM TEMPERATURE
Normal temperature with a winter low of 10°C (50°F). Tolerates high summer heat if roots are kept moist.

💧 WHEN TO WATER
Plants in active growth need regular watering. Keep the compost just moist during winter when growth has stopped.

✋ SURVIVAL STRATEGY
If your houseplants are likely to be affected by whitefly this will be the first plant to get it – be vigilant (see p.187). Feed regularly throughout the growing season.

SIZE
68cm/27in

🏠 SITE
Conservatory

Lavandula x *christiana*

Lavender

Winter is not a time you would expect to have flowering plants around, but given sufficient warmth – around 10–15°C (50–59°F) – and good light, this near-hardy lavender can be made to flower for almost the whole year. The divided grey foliage is soft and feathery, and complements the blue flowers to perfection. The typical lavender flowers are held high on long stalks that may reach 1m (3ft) tall, but are usually much shorter.

HOW MUCH LIGHT
Give as much light as possible, including full sun at all times.

ROOM TEMPERATURE
Tolerates a winter minimum of 2–3°C (36–37°F) but around 16–18°C (61–64°F) is ideal all year.

WHEN TO WATER
This is a drought-tolerant plant that does not enjoy having wet roots. Keep the compost only just moist in winter if temperatures are low. Feed every 3 weeks in summer.

SURVIVAL STRATEGY
This is a vigorous plant that needs space but can be kept compact by clipping back after flowering, or in mid- to late summer. It happily overwinters in a cool environment but lower temperatures will temporarily halt flowering.

SIZE
65cm/26in

SITE
South-facing window

Lotus maculatus

Parrot's beak

This is a native of the Canary Islands and a very showy plant when hung with dozens of its vibrant parrot's-bill flowers. While not in flower it makes a stylish tangle of trailing frizzy grey foliage. Display in a basket or let it dangle from a shelf; a well grown plant will trail 70–80cm (28–32in). Flowers come in waves with the main flush in early summer. *L. berthelotti* is a red-flowered look-alike.

HOW MUCH LIGHT
Provide as much light as possible throughout the year; it will tolerate full direct sun.

ROOM TEMPERATURE
Best at normal room temperature 18–24°C (64–75°F) all year, but takes winter lows of 5–6°C (41–43°F).

WHEN TO WATER
Ensure it stays moist throughout the growing season. Keep it on the dry side when temperatures are low in winter.

SURVIVAL STRATEGY
Regular feeding will encourage flowering. Cut back straggly growth at any time of the year. Ensure that it gets good light during winter.

SIZE
25cm/10in

SITE
Hanging basket

Mandevilla x *amabilis* 'Alice du Pont'

Mandevilla

There are several species of mandevilla, all of which require more or less the same treatment. They are twining climbers: to show them at their best, allow them to meander along a wall on a trellis or wires. Alternatively, keep them quite compact in a pot by pruning back after flowering and wrapping the stems around a frame. *M. laxa* is more cold tolerant and has scented flowers.

HOW MUCH LIGHT
Good light is needed to encourage flowering. Avoid direct scorching sun but otherwise give plenty of light.

ROOM TEMPERATURE
Normal room temperature 18–24°C (64–75°F), with a winter minimum of 15–16°C (59–61°F).

WHEN TO WATER
Water regularly in the growing season. Large plants in small pots will need daily checking in warm weather. Water sparingly in winter but do not allow compost to dry out, as the plant needs moisture to sustain its evergreen leaves.

SURVIVAL STRATEGY
Flowers are produced on the current season's growth, so encourage a greater number of new shoots – and therefore more blooms – by cutting back hard after flowering.

SIZE
45cm/18in

SITE
Conservatory

Maranta leuconeura var. *erythroneura*

Prayer plant

Marantas are very beautiful foliage plants from the tropical woodland floor. Some of their leaf markings are so neat and precise that they look unreal, especially in this red-veined variety. They have a gradually spreading, low-growing habit, and are ideal for growing around the base of taller plants in wide shallow pots where they will enjoy the protection from direct sunlight. Each evening the leaves roll themselves up and stand erect, earning the plant one of its common names, "prayer plant". The flowers – produced on and off from midsummer to autumn – are insignificant and best removed.

Bright red veins resemble herring bones.

HOW MUCH LIGHT
Keep in bright, indirect light, and avoid hot sunshine.

ROOM TEMPERATURE
Maintain a minimum temperature of 16°C (61°F) all year. Match summer heat with higher humidity.

WHEN TO WATER
Keep moist by watering abundantly in summer. Reduce watering when temperatures are low.

SURVIVAL STRATEGY
Marantas do not enjoy dry air: the warmer it is, the more humidity they need. Dust and water stains spoil the look of the foliage so keep them clean using a damp cloth and take care to avoid splashing the leaves with water.

SIZE
77cm/31in

SITE
Shady living room

Monstera deliciosa

Swiss cheese plant

Along with aspidistra this must be the most mocked and clichéd houseplant of all time. But it is still around and for my money it is one of the best and easiest foliage plants available. It is naturally a climber, so do not be surprised if its supporting roots start clambering up your walls. Potentially a big plant, it needs space to be seen at its best – leaves of 60cm (24in) or more across are not unknown. Well grown plants in good light will have deeply lobed leaves perforated with large holes to reduce resistance to high winds – not usually a problem in most homes.

M. deliciosa 'Variegata'

☼ HOW MUCH LIGHT
Good bright light is essential for large healthy leaves but keep out of direct sun in summer.

🌡 ROOM TEMPERATURE
Comfortable room temperature 18–24°C (64–75°F) with a winter minimum of 10°C (50°F).

💧 WHEN TO WATER
Water regularly during the summer growing season. Reduce watering during winter and be sure not to leave it standing in water. The higher the temperature, the greater need for humidity to prevent the tips of its leaves from browning.

✋ SURVIVAL STRATEGY
Keep the leaves clean with a regular wipe over using a damp cloth. In particularly warm weather spray regularly in an effort to raise levels of humidity. Do not be afraid to cut stems back in spring to keep the plant within bounds; sideshoots will soon appear.

SIZE
1.5m/5ft

🏠 SITE
Large bathroom

Display ideas | Plants for bathrooms

Tillandsia cyanea, **p.165**

If you're looking to bring nature indoors, where better to start than your bathroom? Hard, tiled surfaces and functional styling cry out for plants to soften them. It's often the most humid room in the house, which suits a range of plants, and it may be brighter than you think; light entering through the smallest window is maximised when it bounces off tiles and mirrors.

Phalaenopsis, **p.133**

Asplenium nidus, **p.31**

Adiantum capillus-veneris, **p.20**

Soleirolia soleirolii, **p.154**

Musa acuminata 'Dwarf Cavendish'

Banana

You want to grow your own bananas?
Then this is the plant most likely to
provide them, although there is no
guarantee. Even without fruit it is a
handsome leafy specimen whose large
paddle-shaped foliage, often reaching
over 1m (3ft) long, will comfortably
take centre stage. The plant may
grow over 2m (6ft) tall if well
cared for. Consistent, high
temperatures are essential for
fruiting: around 28°C (82°F) is
needed, with a minimum of
about 18°C (64°F) at night.

Textured leaf blades grow to an impressive size.

🌤 HOW MUCH LIGHT
Provide bright filtered light
throughout the year.

🌡 ROOM TEMPERATURE
Normal temperatures will give you a
handsome foliage plant; maintain a
winter minimum of 10°C (50°F).

💧 WHEN TO WATER
Check regularly and keep it well
watered during the growing season.
Reduce watering in winter, but do
not allow it to dry out completely.

✋ SURVIVAL STRATEGY
Enjoys a humid atmosphere. Feed
every week with a balanced liquid
feed during spring and summer.
When cleaning the leaves take care
not to polish off the light bloom that
coats them; use a feather duster.
Shoots that fruit die out but will be
replaced by new ones.

SIZE
70cm/28in

SITE
Conservatory

Nematanthus gregarius

Nematanthus

When young this plant is upright and bushy, but as it grows the stems begin to trail and can eventually spill 60cm (24in) or more out of a pot or hanging basket. The main flowering season is summer, but given sufficient warmth it might produce the occasional flower in winter. The shiny leaves are attractive in their own right.

HOW MUCH LIGHT
Requires bright filtered light all year.

ROOM TEMPERATURE
Happy at room temperature with a minimum of 14°C (57°F) – but winter warmth encourages winter blooms.

WHEN TO WATER
Always use soft water for watering. Keep compost moist but not wet in summer. Water more sparingly during winter when temperatures and light levels are lower.

SURVIVAL STRATEGY
Give it a half-strength balanced liquid feed every 2–3 weeks during the summer months.

SIZE
33cm/13in

SITE
Hanging basket

Nephrolepis exaltata 'Sonata'

Boston fern

Ferns add an air of freshness and coolness, and this one, with its neatly arranged fronds, does the job as well as any. The arching fronds make a dense, luxurious clump that is attractive in its own right, but it also looks good when mixed with foliage plants such as calatheas, asparagus, or ivies (*Hedera*). Remove brown or bent fronds to help keep the plant looking tidy.

🌤 HOW MUCH LIGHT
Keep out of direct midday sun but otherwise place in bright conditions where it can receive plenty of light.

🌡 ROOM TEMPERATURE
Normal room temperature 18–24°C (64–75°F) is adequate, with a winter minimum of 10°C (50°F).

💧 WHEN TO WATER
Use soft water to irrigate and for misting. This leafy plant uses up a lot of water in summer, and so needs regular watering. Dryness at the roots will quickly cause the fronds to turn brown.

✋ SURVIVAL STRATEGY
Plants kept in a warm environment through winter will continue to grow, so check them frequently to see if they need watering; they also enjoy a misting of soft water. Provide a half-strength balanced liquid feed regularly during summer.

📏 SIZE
55cm/22in

🏠 SITE
Bathroom; kitchen

Nertera granadensis
Bead plant

I cannot look at this plant without smiling. The bright orange berries are fighting way above their weight compared to the tiny leaves matted beneath them. The berries start as small, yellowy-green flowers, which are produced in early summer. They develop their orange colour gradually, but persist on the plant for many months. It is easy to grow – and lots of fun.

A white-berried form is also available.

HOW MUCH LIGHT
Give plenty of light including direct sun, but not when it is at its hottest.

ROOM TEMPERATURE
Cool conditions: 14–15°C (57–59°F) is plenty warm enough in summer; winter minimum is 5–6°C (41–43°F).

WHEN TO WATER
Do not let this plant dry out at any time. Keep moist in summer and reduce water during winter. It's easier, but not essential, to water from the bottom.

SURVIVAL STRATEGY
Humidity helps the flowers set and form berries so a daily misting of water will be beneficial during flowering and until berries develop.

SIZE
10cm/4in

SITE
East- or west-facing window

Nolina recurvata syn. *Beaucarnea recurvata*

Elephant foot tree

A curious-looking plant from the semi-desert regions of the southern USA and Mexico. Its large bulbous base supports a woody stem, from which tufts of dark green leaves sprout at the top. Big plants make impressive architectural specimens for conservatories or large well-lit rooms. Provided it receives plenty of light and is not over-watered, this is an easy plant to look after.

HOW MUCH LIGHT
This is a plant of open terrain and therefore needs plenty of light.

ROOM TEMPERATURE
Maintain a winter minimum of 7°C (45°F); year-round, temperatures of 16–20°C (61–68°F) suffice.

WHEN TO WATER
Water regularly during summer and sparingly in winter. It is accustomed to semi-desert conditions so do not allow it to stand in water.

SURVIVAL STRATEGY
Pot into a well drained compost to avoid any chance of waterlogging.

SIZE
1m/3ft

SITE
Conservatory

Olea europaea
Olive

If you long to eat olives from your own plant, prepare to be disappointed. You may well get small fruits developing after the plant has flowered, but there is an elaborate process involving caustic soda that is needed to make them edible. Purely as a foliage plant, its bushy growth and grey-green leathery leaves – which have silvery undersides – make it an attractive and durable evergreen that may stand outside in the garden during the summer months.

Tiny, fragrant flowers appear in summer.

HOW MUCH LIGHT
Ensure full light all year including direct sunlight. Plants kept outdoors in summer benefit from extra light.

ROOM TEMPERATURE
A tough plant that tolerates -2°C (28°F) in winter, but is happy at room temperature for the rest of the year.

WHEN TO WATER
Despite a mental image of scorched dry olive plantations, an adequate supply of water in summer will give you a healthier plant. Keep it dryer in winter.

SURVIVAL STRATEGY
To initiate flowering, olives need at least 2 months of cool temperatures averaging below 10°C (50°F). To maintain a good shape and restrict their size, prune after flowering or during midsummer.

SIZE
90cm/36in

SITE
Conservatory

Pachira aquatica

Malabar chestnut

An imposing architectural plant with large seven-fingered leaves, which is sometimes offered as a specimen with multiple plaited stems. Left alone it would eventually make a small tree, but it is very tolerant of pinching out and pruning back, so there's no difficulty in keeping it compact and within bounds. This is a very easy plant that tolerates considerable neglect, but responds well to proper care. Its flowers produce edible, chestnut-flavoured, multi-seeded fruit (though not always when grown indoors). Although vigorous, even large plants can be accommodated in a 30cm (12in) pot, and it is highly suitable as focal point for a conservatory or living room.

HOW MUCH LIGHT
Give plenty of light including some direct sunlight, but not scorching midday sun.

ROOM TEMPERATURE
Normal room temperature 18–24°C (64–75°F), with a winter minimum of 14°C (57°F).

WHEN TO WATER
The species name refers to its native wetland habitat, but despite its origins it is surprisingly tolerant of the occasional drying out, as long as it is not in direct sun at the same time. For the best growth, water freely in the active summer period then reduce watering in winter.

SURVIVAL STRATEGY
Few plants are less demanding. The biggest problem is controlling its size, but this is easily done by regularly pinching out the growing tips. A fortnightly application of balanced liquid feed in the growing season keeps it healthy.

SIZE
73cm/29in

SITE
Living room; conservatory

Paphiopedilum 'Pinocchio Alba'

Slipper orchid

There are dozens of hybrid slipper orchids of very varied size, colour, and shape. Some are trickier to grow than others, but those most commonly found for sale are generally among the easiest, and the most durable. Flowers usually appear from autumn, through winter, to spring, though flowering plants may be found at almost anytime. Each flower can last for one or two months and with successional opening they can provide a good show for a very long time.

P. 'Pinocchio'

☁ HOW MUCH LIGHT
Keep in lightly shaded conditions and out of bright sunlight.

🌡 ROOM TEMPERATURE
Normal levels, with a winter low of 13°C (55°F); a 3–4 degree drop after flowering helps initiate new flowers.

☕ WHEN TO WATER
For 5–6 weeks after flowering, allow the compost to become almost dry before watering. At other times let compost dry slightly before giving it a 5-minute dunk in soft water and then draining for half an hour before replacing it in its cachepot.

✋ SURVIVAL STRATEGY
Avoid getting water on the foliage as it may cause rotting. Tie floppy flower stems to a cane. Use orchid feed every 3 weeks when watering in summer. Ensure compost is open and very free draining.

🗄 SIZE
40cm/16in

🏠 SITE
Bedroom; bathroom; kitchen

Passiflora 'Lady Margaret'
Passion flower

There are many varieties of passion flower with the potential – despite their vigour – to be grown as houseplants, but usually only *P. caerulea* is offered, and ironically this can be grown outside in all but very cold regions. The flowers on tender varieties like 'Lady Margaret', *P. antioquiensis*, *P. coccinea*, and the flamboyant *P. quadrangularis* are undoubtedly showy and a worthwhile addition to a conservatory planting. To keep plants within bounds you need to cut them back very hard each spring. Main stems can be cut back to just 25cm (10in) or if a framework is established cut side shoots to 3–4cm (1½in). Be brutal! You cannot prune too hard.

P. caerulea

☁ HOW MUCH LIGHT
Give full light to ensure sturdy growth and good flowering.

🌡 ROOM TEMPERATURE
Minimum is 11–15°C (52–59°F) in winter, except for P. caerulea, which tolerates freezing temperatures.

💧 WHEN TO WATER
Leafy passion flowers are very thirsty plants, so regular watering in summer is essential. Water sparingly during winter when growth has stopped.

✋ SURVIVAL STRATEGY
These are vigorous plants that need regular watering and feeding. Train all new long shoots onto a frame or hoop, and keep twining-in shoots as they appear. The tendrils will hold plants on the frame.

📏 SIZE
75cm/30in

🏠 SITE
Conservatory

Pelargonium 'Peggy Sue'

Geranium

There are hundreds upon hundreds of different pelargoniums and though some are chosen for their colourful or scented foliage, many are grown for their propensity to produce brightly coloured flowers for most of the year – given warmth and good light. Regal pelargoniums have some of the largest flowers ranging from almost black, through pink and red, to white, but the most common type – the Zonals, named for the dark zones of their leaves – have large heads of smaller flowers and are very showy.

P. 'Nellie Nuttal'

☼ HOW MUCH LIGHT
Good light is important particularly in winter. Give direct light but avoid the hottest afternoon summer sun.

🌡 ROOM TEMPERATURE
Ideal at room temperature. 18–24°C (64–75°F). If light is poor in winter, keep cool to avoid straggly growth.

☕ WHEN TO WATER
Tolerates the occasional drying out but try to keep moist in summer. If light is good and temperatures are kept up keep watering during winter. Otherwise reduce watering until spring. then repot and begin watering regularly.

✋ SURVIVAL STRATEGY
Look out for whitefly and aphids (see p.187). Remove spent flowers: in moist conditions fallen petals can cause rot on the leaves. Feed regularly. In spring cut hard back to maintain a shapely plant. If you want to propagate them, most root easily from a cutting in a jar of water.

SIZE
40cm/16in

🏠 SITE
Sunny window

Display ideas | Low light conditions

Dracaena fragrans Deremensis Group 'Lemon and Lime', **pp.76–77**

At first sight it may seem impossible to find a plant that will thrive in parts of the house that receive little or no direct light, such as stairwells and hallways. Fortunately some plants – often those with large, dark, or densely packed leaves – have adapted to life beneath bigger neighbours in the wild, and many of them make excellent subjects for the darker corners of your rooms.

Aspidistra elatior, **p.30**

Adiantum capillus-veneris, **p.20**

Monstera deliciosa, **p.115**

Pericallis x *hybrida* Brilliant Series

Florists' cineraria

A traditional flowering houseplant that should be
treated as a short-lived but showy centrepiece then
discarded. Buy a plant in bud, keep it cool and you
will get several weeks of flowering out of it. The
daisy-like flowers are brightly coloured and range
through pink, blue, red, copper, and white; some
have a white eye but others are solid colour.

P. x *hybrida* Spring Glory Series

☁ HOW MUCH LIGHT
Good light is important, but keep out
of direct sunlight; cool conditions are
beneficial.

🌡 ROOM TEMPERATURE
Cool temperatures around 14–16°C
(57–61°F) are ideal and will keep
flowers blooming longer.

💧 WHEN TO WATER
Drying out at any time greatly
reduces the length of the flowering
period; keep the compost constantly
moist but not too wet.

✋ SURVIVAL STRATEGY
If the demands for moisture and
coolness are met then this plant
flowers over a long period. No
feeding is necessary as plants are
discarded. Aphids and whitefly may
be a problem (see p.187).

SIZE
40cm/16in

🏠 SITE
Bright
dining
room

Phalaenopsis cultivars

Moth orchid

For elegant sprays of large flowers borne on strong
arching stems up to 90cm (36in) long, look no further.
There are many hybrids in different shades including
pink, white, and red, with various markings on the
flowers, but all need the same growing conditions.
Epiphytic (tree dwelling) orchids, such as this moth
orchid, have rambling roots that spread across the
surface of the pot and out, searching for nutrients and
support. The roots contain chlorophyll and therefore
produce energy from light, so growing the plants in
open lattice baskets or clear pots is advantageous; you
are also likely to notice if the roots are wet or dry.

Flowers may appear at any time of year.

HOW MUCH LIGHT
Bright light, but not direct sunlight.
Provide plenty of extra artifical light
in winter to encourage flowering.

ROOM TEMPERATURE
Ideally about 20°C (68°F), with high
humidity. Cool nights are important:
allow a dip of around 3–4 degrees.

WHEN TO WATER
Water freely during the growing
season. Reduce watering in winter
and keep almost dry. Plants benefit
from regular spraying with soft
water, but avoid spraying their
flowers. Do not allow water to sit on
the leaves as it may cause rotting,
especially in low temperatures.

SURVIVAL STRATEGY
In summer feed fortnightly with
orchid feed by dunking roots in the
solution for 5 minutes and allowing
to drain. After flowering, cut stem
back to the 2nd lowest bud to to get
a new flowering shoot. Alternatively
remove the old stem completely for
an even more shapely new shoot.

SIZE
62cm/
24½in

SITE
Bathroom

Philodendron erubescens
Philodendron

Philodendrons are among the most dramatic foliage plants. *P. erubescens* has many varieties, some with rich red leaves and others softly suffused with gold. It is sometimes known as "blushing philodendron" from *erubescens* – the Greek for "red". But the most common – and controllable – philodendron is *P. scandens*, the sweetheart vine, named for its large heart-shaped leaves, with stems that will root themselves to a moss pole as they climb. Without support they trail down providing a swathe of rich green foliage. If you want to give a home to the impressive *P. bipinnatifidum,* be sure to give it plenty of space to show its enormous and unusual leaves at their best. Philodendrons are easy plants to grow given just a minimum of care, but look out for scale insects (see p.187).

WATER RESERVES Cut the base off a bottle and prick a tiny hole in the cap to provide enough water for a few days away.

☼ HOW MUCH LIGHT
Keep out of the scorching midday sun but provide good bright light for healthy, well-coloured leaves.

🌡 ROOM TEMPERATURE
Normal room temperature 18–24°C (64–75°F) is adequate, with a winter minimum of 14–15°C (57–59°F).

♒ WHEN TO WATER
When the plant is actively growing water regularly keeping the compost just moist but not wet. When growth slows in winter allow compost to dry out partly before watering sparingly.

✋ SURVIVAL STRATEGY
Keep the leaves clean with a damp cloth to show them at their best. Tie climbing species to a moss pole, keeping the pole moist to encourage the plant's aerial roots to cling. Feed regularly during the summer growing season. Cut back vigorous plants at any time.

⌿ SIZE
1.5m/5ft

⌂ SITE
Bathroom

Other varieties

P. bipinnatifidum Sprouts hefty snakelike ariel roots and dramatic, deeply-lobed leaves up to 1m (3ft) long from a rather squat trunk.

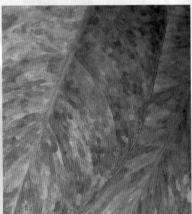

P. domesticum 'Fantasy' Leathery foliage gives this spade-leaved climber, which can reach 6m (20ft), some resistance to low humidity.

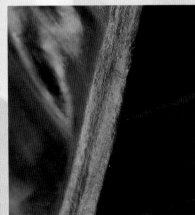

P. 'Imperial Red' A non-climbing variety which gradually reaches 1m (3ft). The deep red leaves turn greener as they age.

◁ *P. scandens* 'Cobra' Keeps its bold stripes even in shady corners, but benefits from a move nearer the window in dark winters.

Phoenix canariensis

Canary Island date palm

An easily-grown palm that develops a rough fibrous rounded base as it matures. The tough leaves are stiff and spiny but beautifully arranged. It's a good conservatory plant but do not expect to get any dates. It tolerates surprisingly cool conditions, and succeeds at near-freezing temperatures if you keep it dry in winter. *P. roebelenii* is a softer, more delicate plant, and does not stand low temperatures.

HOW MUCH LIGHT
The tough leaves of this plant enjoy bright, direct light. Keep it out of shade and in a well lit position.

ROOM TEMPERATURE
Although it withstands cold winters, it grows most satisfactorily at room temperature 18–24°C (64–75°F).

WHEN TO WATER
Water freely during summer when in full growth. Reduce watering in winter, and keep the compost only just moist.

SURVIVAL STRATEGY
Regular feeding during summer keeps the foliage a good dark green colour. The leaves are particularly spiny and anyone with children should be aware of the danger to their eyes.

SIZE
65cm/26in

SITE
Conservatory

Pilea cadierei

Aluminium plant

Pileas are attractive small foliage plants with very diverse leaf shapes and an array of interesting common names. *P. cadierei*, from Vietnam, has robust corrugated leaves with aluminium-silver markings. *P. invloucrata*, the friendship plant, weighs in with strikingly marked, textured foliage. The tiny leaves of the relatively short-lived South American *P. microphylla* give it a fernlike appearance, but it is the flowers that earn it the common name of artillery plant: when mature, they explode, scattering pollen far and wide. All pileas need more or less the same conditions; try them together as a neat foliage group.

P. microphylla

P. involucrata

HOW MUCH LIGHT
Keep out of direct sunlight; partial shade is ideal.

ROOM TEMPERATURE
Avoid high summer temperatures without high humidity; winter minimum is 11–14°C (52–57°F).

WHEN TO WATER
When actively growing keep the compost moist but not wet. At cooler winter temperatures when the plants are dormant, reduce watering and let the compost become partly dry before watering sparingly.

SURVIVAL STRATEGY
Take care: over-watering is a common problem. Apply a balanced liquid feed fortnightly during the summer growing season. Old plants may become straggly and although pinching back the stems can encourage bushiness, they are generally best replaced.

SIZE
18cm/7in

SITE
Table top

Platycerium bifurcatum

Common staghorn fern

This is a curious looking fern whose common name is distinctly apt. It normally grows up in trees in relatively high humidity and at warm temperatures so it is slightly demanding in its needs, but when grown well, a large specimen is a striking sight. It bears two types of frond. One supports the plant on the tree and spreads from the base of the plant and eventually turns brown. The other provides the erect grey-green "leaves".

HOW MUCH LIGHT
It enjoys bright light, but avoid placing it in hot, direct sun without providing high humidity.

ROOM TEMPERATURE
Room temperatures of 18–24°C (64–75°F) are sufficient, with a winter minimum of 13°C (55°F).

WHEN TO WATER
The flat supporting frond tends to spread over the pot making it almost impossible to check for dryness and difficult to water from the top. Dunk it in a bowl when it shows signs of drooping, and allow to drain. Reduce watering in winter to a quick dip.

SURVIVAL STRATEGY
Give it a half-strength balanced liquid feed every month throughout summer, Stop feeding during winter. Regular misting and high humidity will be beneficial. Any dust should be blown off the fronds because attempts to wipe it off will remove their fine covering of down.

SIZE
35cm/14in

SITE
Hanging basket

Plumbago auriculata

Cape leadwort

Here is a plant of great charm and lightness. It is a vigorous scrambling plant with light green leaves and open heads of pale blue flowers that are produced throughout the summer. Ideally it needs the space of a conservatory, where its long shoots can be given some elbow room; otherwise, wrap the shoots around a wire frame or tie them in to a trellis. It flowers on the current season's growth so prune it back to a framework of mature branches in spring to promote new flowering shoots.

HOW MUCH LIGHT
This plant needs plenty of light and will take full sun as long as it is kept moist at the roots.

ROOM TEMPERATURE
Benefits from winter temperatures of around 10°C (50°F). Provide maximum light for warmer winters.

WHEN TO WATER
Keep the plant moist – but not waterlogged – throughout summer. Keep it dryer during the winter resting period.

SURVIVAL STRATEGY
This is a self-reliant plant which should perform well as long as it is fed regularly with a balanced liquid feed and given plenty of light. Removing the long shoots during summer will reduce flowering, so cut them off in early spring. Check for whitefly occasionally (see p.187).

SIZE
55cm/22in

SITE
Conservatory: south-facing window

Pteris cretica 'Alexandrae'
Cretan brake

Pteris are striking and elegant ferns, with their fronds usually held on thin, erect stems giving the plants an air of elegance and openness. Their requirements are minimal and they make very reliable houseplants. The tall stems and splayed fronds of 'Alexandrae' lend it the appearance – and all the appeal – of a wayward firework. Set it against a light background to show off its shapely silhouette.

Crested tips add an alien touch to the fronds.

HOW MUCH LIGHT
Keep out of direct sun but provide bright filtered light all year round.

ROOM TEMPERATURE
Withstands winter lows of 2–3°C (36–37°F). Keep humidity levels high in hot summer conditions.

WHEN TO WATER
Keep moist throughout the growing season. Reduce watering slightly during periods of low temperature but do not allow it to dry out.

SURVIVAL STRATEGY
Apply a fortnightly dose of balanced liquid feed. In warm temperatures maintain high humidity by standing the plant on a tray of moist pebbles, and spraying regularly (see p.178).

SIZE
60cm/24in

SITE
Bathroom

Punica granatum var. nana

Dwarf pomegranate

This is a small version of the pomegranate and although it may produce tiny fruits late in the season, they are really not edible. Its main attraction is its bright orange flowers that are produced over a long period from early summer to autumn. It is a deciduous plant; after it has lost its leaves keep it cool at around 10°C (50°F). A good plant for the conservatory.

HOW MUCH LIGHT
This is a plant that normally enjoys a Mediterranean climate, so provide maximum light during summer.

ROOM TEMPERATURE
Accepts normal temperatures 18–24°C (64–75°F) in summer; ideal winter levels are around 10°C (50°F).

WHEN TO WATER
Keep the compost moist during the summer. In winter keep just moist enough to prevent it drying out.

SURVIVAL STRATEGY
Feed regularly during summer. As it has no leaves in winter, and therefore little need for light, you can tuck it away out of sight until growth begins again in spring.

SIZE
40cm/16in

SITE
South-facing window

Rhapis excelsa

Miniature fan palm

A bushy, elegant palm from sub-tropical China and Japan. In its natural habitat it endures the low light levels of the forest floor, which means it tolerates a shady position in the home. Each leaf is made up of between five and eight flattened fanlike segments. Suckers spread throughout the pot to make an impressive thicket of leafy stems. There are variegated forms available too: 'Variegata' has white striped leaves, and 'Zuikonishiki' is smaller (to 60cm/24in) with yellow variegation.

HOW MUCH LIGHT
Filtered light or place it by a window that does not receive direct sunlight.

ROOM TEMPERATURE
A winter minimum of 8–10°C (46–50°F), and summers of 18–25°C (64–75°F) keep it growing strongly.

WHEN TO WATER
Water regularly during the growing season, and when temperatures are high, but reduce watering if the temperature falls during the winter months. Provide higher humidity in warm conditions.

SURVIVAL STRATEGY
Pull off unsightly and browning leaves. Pulling rather than cutting off the leaves exposes an attractive leaf scar and some of the smooth stem beneath the fibre covering. Apply a fortnightly balanced liquid feed during summer.

SIZE
1.2m/3½ft

SITE
Hallway

Rhododendron simsii

Azalea

When it comes to sheer flower power there are few plants to rival the azalea. At its peak the flowers can completely obliterate the foliage, especially if kept in a cool spot. After flowering, and once all danger of frost has passed, this evergreen shrub may be put outside for summer in a sheltered shady place. Bring it back into the house before the first autumn frosts.

HOW MUCH LIGHT
Keep in bright light but out of direct sunlight.

ROOM TEMPERATURE
Keep it cool, and flowers last longer: ideally 10–16°C (50–61°F) in bloom. Avoid temperatures over 24°C (75°F).

WHEN TO WATER
This is an ericaceous (lime-hating) plant, which means it needs soft water. If the pot is bursting to the brim with compost and roots, it is better to dunk the whole thing rather than attempt to water from above. Do not let it dry out.

SURVIVAL STRATEGY
Repot plants in ericaceous compost before placing outdoors for summer. Do not neglect them once they're outside: regular watering and a liquid feed specifically formulated for lime-hating plants are essential.

SIZE
33cm/14in

SITE
East-facing window

Ananas comosus var. *variegatus*, **p.27**

THE BRIGHT CONDITIONS of a conservatory can be a haven for houseplants; if you provide the right environment, you can create an exotic indoor garden to enjoy all year. Conservatories may get extremely hot if they are not ventilated in summer; few plants tolerate such extremes without being scorched and frizzled, and even drought-tolerant plants need at least some water in the heat.

Dracaena marginata, **pp.76–77**

Passiflora caerulea, **p.126**

Brugmansia candida, **p.38**; *Olea europea*, **p.123**; x *Citrofortunella microcarpa*, **p.55**

Saintpaulia cultivars
African violet

Ask anyone to name three houseplants and the
chances are that this will be one of them. African
violets seem to have been around from the year
dot, and the hybridisers have been hard at work
ever since, producing varieties with double, frilled,
ruffled, and bicoloured flowers in pinks, blues, and
whites, and pretty well every shade in between.
There are also plants with variegated foliage.

'Dorothy'   'Fancy pants'

'Porcelain'   'Mina'

🌤 HOW MUCH LIGHT
Good light is needed for continuous
flowering, but avoid direct sunlight.

🌡 ROOM TEMPERATURE
Even levels of 17–23°C (63–73°F) are
best. Cold draughts and fluctuating
temperatures prevent flowering.

💧 WHEN TO WATER
Water from the bottom and allow to
drain. The plant's roots are in danger
of rotting if the compost is kept too
wet, so allow it to dry out slightly
between waterings. The cooler the
temperature, the dryer the compost
should be.

🖐 SURVIVAL STRATEGY
Rotting in the heart of the plant is
always a risk. Do not allow the
crown to get wet, and always remove
spent flowers. Pull off any damaged
foliage but ensure that you do not
leave any stubs that are likely to rot.

SIZE
20cm/8in

🏠 SITE
Bright
table top

Sansevieria trifasciata 'Laurentii'

Mother-in-law's tongue

S. trifasciata is originally from central Africa and closely related to spiky agaves. It is so easy to grow that it has acquired something of a reputation for being dull and uninteresting, and its common name has certainly not helped. Do not be fooled: it's a useful and attractive foliage plant that may even give you flowers if it gets a long warm summer and good light. And although they are produced erratically, the lax spikes of greenish-white flowers have a sweet night time fragrance well worth waiting for. Several variously shaped and coloured cultivars have arisen making it ideal for the enthusiast to start a small, easily cared for collection.

MAKING MORE TONGUES Propagate by easing apart the rootstock and cutting through it with a sharp knife. Plant the offsets in free-draining compost and a pot that provides good drainage.

HOW MUCH LIGHT
Enjoys bright light and takes full sun if kept moist. In winter give as much light as possible.

ROOM TEMPERATURE
Most comfortable at around 18–25°C (64–77°F), but no lower than 11–12°C (52–54°F) in winter.

WHEN TO WATER
Keep compost moist, but not wet, when in active growth. During dormancy keep it almost dry: allow compost to dry out before watering moderately. Do not get water into the heart of the plant. Cold conditions may cause the leaves to rot at the base, particularly if over-watered.

SURVIVAL STRATEGY
Practically indestructible, unless it's over-watered. This is a slow-growing plant and deep shade will make it slower still. Wipe the leaves clean with a damp cloth. Only repot when pot bound. Propagate by division or leaf cuttings – but leaf cuttings will lose their variegation.

SIZE
78cm/31in

SITE
Minimalist interior

Schefflera arboricola

Umbrella tree

Although slightly more diminutive than the equally common *S. actinophylla*, this umbrella tree displays all the toughness of its big brother. Its leathery foliage, held on umbrella-style stalks, makes it resistant to dry air and even to the occasional drying out. The variegated leaves of this variety lighten the otherwise rather gloomy dark green of its foliage. Its growth is naturally upright: pinch out the shoot tips to keep it bushy. This is a reliable plant that seems to tolerate a degree of neglect.

GOOD GROOMING Keep the foliage clean to get healthier plants; mucky leaves collect less light and so provide less energy. Wipe the leaves clean with a damp cloth, supporting them from below.

HOW MUCH LIGHT
Needs good light conditions, but not direct hot summer sun.

ROOM TEMPERATURE
Normal room temperature 18–24°C (64–75°F) is sufficient. Warmer conditions require greater humidity.

WHEN TO WATER
Keep moist during the growing season. Reduce watering during winter but do not allow the compost to dry out completely.

SURVIVAL STRATEGY
Feed every fortnight with a balanced liquid feed during the growing season. Large, leggy plants can be cut back by half in spring to stimulate bushy sideshoots.

SIZE
45cm/18in

SITE
Living room

Schlumbergera hybrids

Christmas cactus

This popular cactus, with spreading foliage and successive, pendulous flowers, is a cross between *S. truncata* and *S. russelliana*. Further hybridising has led to more colours including white, orange, and yellow. For good flowering, provide long nights of uninterrupted darkness – which means no artificial light – in autumn. Blooms often appear in late winter, so don't panic if you wake up to find there are none open on Christmas Day.

HOW MUCH LIGHT
Keep out of scorching summer sun but give lots of light in winter. If plant is turned, buds may drop (see p.179).

ROOM TEMPERATURE
Normal room temperature 18–24°C (64–75°F) is ideal all year. Plants in bloom last longer in cooler rooms.

WHEN TO WATER
Use soft water to help maintain slightly acidic conditions. Keep on the dry side for a few weeks after flowering then water regularly so that compost remains moist but is not waterlogged. Provide a high potash feed every 3–4 weeks in summer.

SURVIVAL STRATEGY
Draughts, over-watering and cold temperatures can cause buds to drop. Keep hybrids above 15°C (59°F) to hold their colour. In temperate climates plants can be put outside in summer but keep out of direct sun. Use open, free-draining ericaceous (lime-free) compost.

SIZE
45cm/18in

SITE
Hanging basket

Sedum morganianum

Donkey's tail

This is a deliciously chunky succulent with a relaxed attitude to life, as it lolls out of its pot and hangs in grey, ever-lengthening dreadlocks that may reach 60–70cm (24–28in). To make the most of its shape, let it drip from a hanging basket. The grey coating is encouraged by direct sun and gives the plant its attractive matt finish. Be careful how you handle it as the fleshy leaf segments come off easily when touched.

HOW MUCH LIGHT
Provide full sunlight to ensure compact growth. Good winter light is important.

ROOM TEMPERATURE
Normal room temperature 18–24°C (64–75°F). Tolerates cooler winters, but keep above 10°C (50°F).

WHEN TO WATER
During summer water regularly letting the compost dry out slightly between waterings. Never leave it standing in water. In winter reduce watering and let the compost become almost dry before giving just a moderate amount of water.

SURVIVAL STRATEGY
This is an easy and straightforward plant to care for. Give it a balanced liquid feed every month during the growing period. The fleshy leaves are likely to root and develop into new plants if stood base down on the surface of compost that is just moist.

SIZE
30cm/12in

SITE
Pedestal table

Selaginella martensii 'Watsoniana'
Selaginella

Here is a plant with something of a split personality.
It looks like a fern but it isn't one; yet to confuse
matters, it produces spores – just like a fern.
Despite its quandary it's an easy and fun plant to
grow. Its fronds arch out, sending down roots
as they spread, which makes it useful for
tucking into big pots or amongst large
groups of plants to provide
groundcover. It also makes a neat
single specimen for a shady corner.

Feather-like leaves create a fluffy textured effect.

☼ HOW MUCH LIGHT
Selaginella enjoys a semi-shaded
position out of direct sunlight.

🌡 ROOM TEMPERATURE
Normal levels 18–24°C (64–75°F) are
fine. It likes a humid atmosphere:
the leaves will shrivel in hot, dry air.

💧 WHEN TO WATER
Keep the compost moist but not wet.
Use soft water. In warm conditions
the plant will grow throughout the
year and need constant watering.
Where winter temperatures are
cooler watering may be reduced but
never let the compost dry out
because the leaves will shrivel.

✋ SURVIVAL STRATEGY
This plant suffers in dry conditions
so regular misting with water at
room temperature is appreciated.
Rooted fronds may be split off to
form new plants at almost any time
of the year.

SIZE
30cm/12in

🏠 SITE
Bathroom;
kitchen

Senecio macroglossus 'Variegatus'

Cape ivy

If at first glance you mistake this for an ivy, you
are forgiven. It climbs or trails just like ivy but a
closer look reveals that, unlike ivy, it has
shiny succulent leaves, and – unlike ivy –
it climbs by twining its stems around
its support. It is a handsome plant
with strong variegation that contrasts
well with the dark stems. Given a framework to
scale it reaches 70cm (28in) or more in height;
equally it will trail down a similar distance if
allowed to spill from a shelf or hanging basket.
Its cousin, *S. rowleyanus,* is a strikingly different
character, with no upwardly mobile aspirations
whatsoever: its strings of green beads simply
hang vertically from its pot.

S. rowleyanus (String of beads)

☼ HOW MUCH LIGHT
Both senecios need good light and
benefit from some direct sunlight,
but not hot, afternoon summer sun.

🌡 ROOM TEMPERATURE
Anywhere between 14–22°C
(57–72°F) is suitable, with a winter
minimum of 10°C (50°F).

💧 WHEN TO WATER
When plants are actively growing –
from spring to late summer – water
regularly, allowing compost to dry
slightly before the next watering.
Reduce watering during the cooler
months and take care to avoid
over-watering.

✋ SURVIVAL STRATEGY
To keep S. macroglossus within
bounds either train the stems
around a framework or pinch out the
shoot tips. S. rowleyanus can be left
to hang: simply cut off the stems
when they are too long. Shoots of
both will root easily when tucked
into the compost surface.

📏 SIZE
51cm/20in

🏠 SITE
Table top;
hanging
basket

Solanum pseudocapsicum

Christmas cherry

A bright and cheerful plant that is at its most interesting when the berries are changing colour and it carries a mixed display of green, yellow and orange fruits. It is also a tough plant that will provide winter colour for many seasons. The berries may tempt children, but they are toxic and must not be eaten, so keep your plant well out of the reach of young fists. Dwarf varieties reach about 30cm (12in) but left unpruned, the full-size species reaches 1m (3ft) or more in height.

HOW MUCH LIGHT
Enjoys a spell outside in summer, where it will benefit from full light. Keep it out of scorching midday sun.

ROOM TEMPERATURE
No need for heat: happy with normal levels of 18–24°C (64–75°F), and a winter minimum of 10°C (50°F).

WHEN TO WATER
Keep well watered and provide a regular application of balanced liquid feed throughout its life. Reduce watering and stop feeding for several weeks when berries wither in late winter, to give the plant a rest.

SURVIVAL STRATEGY
Regular daily misting when in flower helps ensure a good crop of berries. After the late winter dormant period, cut back by one third, repot, and place outside when the danger of frost has passed. Pinch out growing tips to encourage bushy growth.

SIZE
36cm/14in

SITE
Bright table top display

Soleirolia solerolii 'Aurea'

Mind-your-own-business

This is a tiny and easy plant with a great deal of charm. Its
spreading mat or bun of closely-packed leaves is ideal for
simple arrangements, or as groundcover on the pots of larger
plants and in conservatory beds. You can control its expansive
nature by simply cutting it back with scissors, or on large
plants by pulling out shoots by hand. 'Aurea' is one of two
colour variants on the species; the other is 'Variegata', and
both are ever ready to revert to plain green, so cut out any
reverted shoots straight away – a fiddly but necessary job.

S. soleirolii 'Variegata'

S. soleirolii

☇ HOW MUCH LIGHT
Good light will keep plants compact,
but avoid direct sun which is likely to
scorch the foliage.

🌡 ROOM TEMPERATURE
Takes -5°C (23°F); high temperatures
will cause it to become leggy. Ideally
keep cool, around 10–16°C (50–61°F).

💧 WHEN TO WATER
Keep the compost moist. The foliage
will quickly turn brown if it the plant
dries out. Higher temperatures
demand greater humidity.

✋ SURVIVAL STRATEGY
Beyond ensuring it does not dry out
this little plant requires little
attention. To make new plants, dig
out a small section with a spoon and
place it in a pot of fresh compost.
Kept cool and moist it will soon
establish itself and start filling out.

▯ SIZE
18cm/7in

⌂ SITE
North-
facing
windowsill

Solenostemon Wizard Series

Coleus

The old name, *Coleus*, is less of a tongue twister, and is still widely used. They are among the most startling foliage plants around, and regularly go in and out of fashion. The colour range covers red, orange, yellow, every shade of green, pink, copper, and almost black. The shape and patterning of the leaves is almost infinitely varied. There are over a hundred named varieties but they're usually offered in unnamed mixed selections. Pay your money and take your choice.

S. 'Inky Fingers'

HOW MUCH LIGHT
Despite their sometimes fragile appearance they tolerate full sun as long as they are moist at the roots.

ROOM TEMPERATURE
Normal temperature. with a winter minimum of 11–12°C (52–54°F). Low temperatures may cause leaf drop.

WHEN TO WATER
These are leafy plants that need a lot of water in warm conditions and should be checked regularly. Keep the compost moist. Reduce watering in lower temperatures. Take great care not to over-water.

SURVIVAL STRATEGY
Feed fortnightly with a balanced liquid feed. Coleus flowers are insignificant and best pinched out before they develop. Pinch out shoot tips too. to encourage branching and a bushy shape. Summer cuttings root easily in a jar of water.

SIZE
32cm/13in

SITE
East- or west-facing window

Sollya heterophylla

Bluebell creeper

An evergreen plant with small but pretty flowers that are produced all summer long. More of a scrambler than a climber, you will need to entice it through a trellis or a wire frame if you want it to get tall. In a conservatory you can use it to mask the bare legs of taller plants such as bougainvilleas. The flowers are followed by fleshy cylindrical seed pods which are edible, but not particularly tasty.

The bell-shaped flowers may last until autumn.

HOW MUCH LIGHT
Give it a well-lit position in full sun.

ROOM TEMPERATURE
It is almost hardy, and will survive 2–3°C (36–37°F). In summer normal room temperature is sufficient.

WHEN TO WATER
Keep moist in summer. In winter when temperatures are low, reduce watering.

SURVIVAL STRATEGY
Feed fortnightly with a balanced liquid feed. Large plants can be pruned hard and repotted in spring to keep them within bounds and to rejuvenate them.

SIZE
80cm/32in

SITE
Hanging basket; conservatory

Sparrmannia africana

African hemp

Sparrmannia has two valuable attributes. One is its large, downy, pale green leaves; the other is its early season blooms. The white flowers have clusters of red and yellow stamens, which close together quite rapidly when touched by an insect (or a pencil point). It's a large plant with the potential to fill a big space but you can keep it within bounds by regular pruning and shaping.

HOW MUCH LIGHT
Keep in good bright light but avoid scorching midday sun.

ROOM TEMPERATURE
Tolerates cool winter temperatures down to 7°C (45°F). Avoid exposure to high temperatures in summer.

WHEN TO WATER
Large plants will use a lot of water and may need watering daily in warm weather. Reduce watering during the winter rest period.

SURVIVAL STRATEGY
Because of its vigorous growth and large leaves it needs regular feeding and watering to keep it healthy. Fortunately it is tolerant of quite severe pruning, and cutting a large plant back to 30–40cm (12–16in) in spring will not harm it. Prone to whitefly (see p.187).

SIZE
68cm/27in

SITE
Cool conservatory

*Agave attenuata, **p.23***

THERE'S NO ARGUING that plants in porches or hallways provide a friendly, welcoming touch, but often a blast from an open door or draughts through ill-fitting windows cause them to catch their death. Choose tough plants to cope with these conditions – succulents from deserts accustomed to cold nights, or hardy plants that tolerate frost – in order to keep the warmth in your welcome.

Sparrmannia africana, **p.157**

Tolmiea menziesii 'Taff's Gold', **p.166**

Cordyline australis, **p.58**

Spathiphyllum wallisii
Peace lily

Originally this was best known as a foliage plant that
tolerated deep shade. More recently it has attracted
the attention of breeders intent on developing
varieties that produce more flowers. Peace lilies
come in a surprising range of sizes: some make 1m
(3ft) or more in height; others remain resolutely
under 30cm (12in). Spring is their natural flowering
time but, given the right conditions, the white flowers
may appear on and off throughout the year.

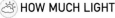
Tiny flowers surround the central spike (spadix).

HOW MUCH LIGHT
Keep lightly shaded in summer, and
out of direct sunlight, but move to
good light in winter.

ROOM TEMPERATURE
Provide a winter minimum of 16°C
(61°F) and avoid the excess heat of a
conservatory in summer.

WHEN TO WATER
During active growth from spring to
autumn keep the compost moist. In
winter water sparingly, letting the
compost dry slightly before watering.

SURVIVAL STRATEGY
Peace lilies enjoy as much humidity
as you can give them. Do not expect
them to flower continually, but
provide plenty of winter light to
encourage good flowering in spring.
Some very large-leaved varieties are
grown for their foliage and are poor
flowerers indoors.

SIZE
48cm/19in

SITE

Kitchen;
bedroom

Stephanotis floribunda

Madagascar jasmine

This is an evergreen climber with hearty, thick, leathery leaves and extremely fragrant flowers that are produced throughout spring and summer. When well grown it can reach over 2m (6ft) tall trained up, for example, a conservatory wall. However it is easily contained in a smaller space by twining or looping its shoots around a wooden or wire framework secured in the pot.

The star-shaped flowers are deliciously scented.

HOW MUCH LIGHT
Give bright light but keep out of direct sun.

ROOM TEMPERATURE
Even temperatures of 20°C (68°F) are ideal. The higher the temperature, the greater the need for humidity.

WHEN TO WATER
Keep the compost moist when the plant is actively growing. Reduce watering during the winter months, allowing the compost to dry slight between waterings, but do not allow it to become completely dry.

SURVIVAL STRATEGY
If necessary, cut back long shoots after flowering. Stephanotis is sensitive to changes of temperature and low humidity so do your best to maintain constant conditions. Regular misting is beneficial.

SIZE
65cm/26in

SITE
Living room; well-ventilated conservatory

Streptocarpus hybrids
Cape primrose

The majority of streptocarpus offered for sale are large-flowered hybrids, although you may occasionally come across species such as *S. saxorum*, whose trailing stems carry small, almost round leaves and attractive flowers, or the extraordinary *S. wenlandii* with one huge leaf up to 70cm (28in) long – but be warned, this plant dies after flowering. The hybrids come in a wide range of colours including white, pink, blue, and rich ruby, and are among the prettiest and gentlest of houseplants.

⊛ HOW MUCH LIGHT
Provide good light, but not direct sunlight.

🌡 ROOM TEMPERATURE
Normal room temperature will keep the plants in flower all year round. Flowering stops below 13°C (55°F).

☝ WHEN TO WATER
Water freely during the warmer months, allowing the top of the compost to dry out between each watering. Water sparingly when temperatures are low.

✋ SURVIVAL STRATEGY
Standing the plant on a tray of damp pebbles to raise humidity will help prevent the leaves browning due to dry air (see p.178). Provide a half-strength high potash liquid feed every 3–4 weeks. Remove spent flowers to encourage more blooms.

📏 SIZE
25cm/10in

🏠 SITE
Table top display

Stromanthe sanguinea 'Tricolor'

Stromanthe

Carrying its leaves at a jaunty, almost horizontal angle, this is a plant which exudes confidence. Its other chief attraction comes from the vibrant red leaf undersides, which contrast well with the mottled upper surfaces. Keep the foliage clean to make the most of the glossy surface. You can split the eventual thicket of shoots in spring; pot them up to provide new plants.

Leaf undersides are streaked with red.

HOW MUCH LIGHT
Keep out of direct light. Bright filtered light is ideal.

ROOM TEMPERATURE
Normal temperature is adequate. High temperatures without humidity will cause leaf browning.

WHEN TO WATER
Keep the compost moist in the growing season but ease off during winter, allowing the compost to dry slightly before watering.

SURVIVAL STRATEGY
During the growing season, apply a half-strength balanced liquid feed every fortnight. Cool, semi-shaded conditions help the plant cope with low humidity. Warmer temperatures would encourage faster growth but necessitate higher humidity.

SIZE
47cm/19in

SITE
Hallway

Syngonium podophyllum

Goosefoot plant

The tall, gangly original plain green form of goosefoot is rarely seen, having been replaced by a range of compact plants with various variegated leaf patterns. The speckled varieties remind me of leaves affected by red spider mite – which keeps me sitting on the fence regarding this plant. The leaves of mature specimens become divided and lobed, providing much more visual interest. All syngoniums enjoy plenty of humidity.

HOW MUCH LIGHT
Bright filtered light. Keep out of direct sunlight.

ROOM TEMPERATURE
Normal room temperature 18–24°C (64–75°F). Requires higher humidity in warmer temperatures.

WHEN TO WATER
Keep the compost moist all year round but allow it to dry slightly between each watering.

SURVIVAL STRATEGY
Grow up a moss pole or let it trail from a shelf or basket. Feed regularly when in growth. If your houseplants are prone to red spider mite. check this plant carefully as the leaf patterns resemble the symptoms of mite infestation and may mask an attack (see p.187).

SIZE
33cm/13in

SITE
Hanging basket; bright shelf

Tillandsia cyanea

Pink quill

A curious but striking plant. The flowerhead is flattened into a fan-like arrangement and the flowers emerge from between the "scales" or overlapping bracts. Up to 20 flowers appear individually, and while each is short-lived, they are produced over a long period, sometimes lasting 10 weeks. Once flowering is finished the rosette of leaves bearing the flower spike dies. It is replaced by offshoots, which may be used for propagation, or left to mature and flower on the plant.

DRIP FEEDING Tillandsias have sparse roots, which are just enough to anchor the plant. Water and nutrients are also taken in by the leaves, which means that they will benefit from regular misting.

HOW MUCH LIGHT
Grow in good light but out of direct scorching sunshine.

ROOM TEMPERATURE
A year round temperature of 18–25°C (64–77°F) is ideal, but tolerates a winter minimum of 14°C (57°F).

WHEN TO WATER
Waterlogging means certain death, so a free-draining compost and pot are crucial. In warmer months either mist frequently so water runs down into compost, or, when it is almost dry, dunk it in soft water at room temperature and drain thoroughly. Water sparingly in winter.

SURVIVAL STRATEGY
During the growing season it benefits from a monthly application of a quarter-strength balanced liquid feed applied either via a misting spray or in the dunking water. Provide as humid an atmosphere as possible.

SIZE
26cm/10in

SITE
Bathroom

Tolmiea menziesii 'Taff's Gold'

Thousand mothers

This is a perfectly hardy plant and an attractive and established favourite for cool and shady conditions. It owes its common name to the young plants that form at the point where the stalk meets the leaf blade. If you detach these with the leaf they will root and form new plants when pressed into the compost surface. The tall flower stalks may bear small flowers but if flowers are produced at all indoors, they are best removed to keep the plant looking neat and tidy.

⚙ HOW MUCH LIGHT
Suits bright filtered light to semi-shade. Low light levels and warm conditions lead to straggly growth.

🌡 ROOM TEMPERATURE
Keep cool; this hardy plant is used to an outdoor life, so high indoor winter temperatures cause drawn growth.

💧 WHEN TO WATER
Keep the compost moist throughout the growing season.

✋ SURVIVAL STRATEGY
Outside, tolmieas would normally experience a cold winter period, therefore they benefit from a few weeks of cooler temperatures when grown indoors.

📏 SIZE
20cm/8in

🏠 SITE
North- or east-facing window

Tradescantia spathacea syn. *Rhoeo discolor*

Three-men-in-a-boat

The robust shape of this plant is not what you might expect from a tradescantia – the name is more often associated with small-leaved trailers – but a glance at the flowers confirms the relationship. Young plants start out sitting on the compost with an erect rosette of stiff leaves, but as they mature the lower leaves are lost and a stem begins to develop.

White flowers cradled at the centre of the plant.

☼ HOW MUCH LIGHT
Enjoys bright light, but keep out of direct sun which may scorch the leaves.

🌡 ROOM TEMPERATURE
Normal room temperature 18–24°C (64–75°F) is adequate, with a winter minimum of 16–17°C (61–63°F).

☔ WHEN TO WATER
Water regularly keeping the compost moist but not wet during the growing period. Keep only just moist during cooler winter months. Over-watering in winter will cause the roots and stem to rot.

✋ SURVIVAL STRATEGY
Good humidity is important to avoid browned leaves or leaf tips. Group with other plants, or stand it on a tray of damp pebbles (see p.178). The higher the temperature, the greater the amount of humidity needed. Feed regularly during the spring and summer growing season.

📏 SIZE
52cm/21in

🏠 SITE
Bright living room

Tradescantia zebrina
Wandering Jew

A delightful, easy-to-grow plant that can be trained up a small frame or allowed to spill out of its pot and trail downwards. The leaves are marked with two silver stripes – which catch the light with a sparkling glint – and their purple undersides create a perfect contrast. And for bonus points, it will occasionally produce small pink flowers.

Stripy silvery-green leaves are purple beneath.

HOW MUCH LIGHT
Bright light will give you the best leaf colouring and encourage flowering, but avoid direct scorching sunlight.

ROOM TEMPERATURE
Normal room temperature 18–24°C (64–75°F) is ideal with a minimum of 12°C (54°F) in winter.

WHEN TO WATER
Keep compost moist when actively growing. Water less in winter, but do not allow it to dry out.

SURVIVAL STRATEGY
Long trailing shoots may lose their leaves and become straggly at the base. Either pinch out the growing tips to keep the plant bushy, or tuck the trailing shoots back into the pot where they will root and form a new plant with fresh leaves. Feed regularly in summer.

SIZE
35cm/14in

SITE
Hanging basket

Vriesea splendens

Flaming sword

Surely one of the most striking plants for the home. The broad, slightly rolled leaves are banded deep purple with shiny undersides that gleam like richly polished wood. The scarlet flower spike is held atop a sturdy stem, and colourful bracts are tightly pressed together in a flattened flowerhead; even if small yellow flowers failed to squeeze themselves from between the bracts, the brilliant spike would still carry the day. The spike lasts for many weeks but eventually turns brown; cut it off near the base. It's much tougher than the exotic appearance suggests, being happy at room temperature, and easily maintained.

DRINKING CUP The centre of the plant forms a remarkably watertight cup, which you should top up at regular intervals throughout the plant's growing season.

HOW MUCH LIGHT
For good leaf colour and flowers it needs bright light with 2–3 hours of direct sun, but not scorching heat.

ROOM TEMPERATURE
When in growth 18–28°C (64–82°F) is ideal, with a winter minimum of 15°C (59°F). Keep humidity high.

WHEN TO WATER
Water regularly into the central cup formed by the leaves and keep the compost moist when the plant is actively growing. In cooler periods of the year, when growth is slowed, keep compost just moist. Be careful not to over-water at this time.

SURVIVAL STRATEGY
During the growing season provide a half-strength balanced liquid feed every month. Pot into orchid mix or free-draining compost. Rosettes that have flowered will die back over a period of several months. Offsets produced from the leaf axils will take the place of the withering rosette.

SIZE
70cm/28in

SITE
East- or west-facing window

Yucca elephantipes
Yucca

An impressive plant with a very strong shape that stands well in its own space, adding an assertive presence to your room. You can buy them as young plants with virtually no stem, or as more mature specimens, which have distinctive shoots branching out of tall sections of rooted trunklike stems. The yucca is a good plant for a well-lit conservatory where it will tolerate both the direct sunlight of summer and the coolness of winter.

Y. elephantipes 'Variegata'

HOW MUCH LIGHT
Provide full light throughout the year.

ROOM TEMPERATURE
Best at room temperature 18–24°C (64–75°F) with a winter minimum of between 8–10°C (46–50°F).

WHEN TO WATER
Keep moderately moist during the active growing period in summer. Reduce watering when temperatures are lower in winter.

SURVIVAL STRATEGY
Keep the plant tidy by carefully pulling, rather than cutting, old leaves from the plant. Feed regularly when in active growth. Yuccas may be placed outside during summer.

SIZE
1.3m/4½ft

SITE
Conservatory

Zamioculcas zamiifolia

Zamioculcas

Here is an East African plant with something of an identity crisis: it looks like a fern, a cycad, and a succulent all rolled into one. The upright growth, dark green colouring, and distinctive shape add up to a striking houseplant, and its tolerance of shade makes it even more useful around the home. Try using zamioculcas as a foil for bolder variegated or flowering plants, or to provide structure in arrangements with fluffy companions like *Asparagus densiflorus*. In its natural habitat it produces green and white flowers, but you're unlikely to see them when you grow it inside.

HOW MUCH LIGHT
Tolerates quite deep shade, but grows better in bright filtered light, away from direct scorching sun.

ROOM TEMPERATURE
This plant grows all year round, so maintain a winter minimum of 15–18°C (59–64°F) and keep it moist.

WHEN TO WATER
Keep the compost moist all year round, apply a balanced liquid feed monthly during summer, and it will grow away with little attention.

SURVIVAL STRATEGY
This is a very easy-going plant that survives on only basic care. It will tolerate the occasional drought, but is likely to shed its leaflets when dry. However, if these fallen leaflets are then laid on moist compost they produce roots, and within 2 years you will have small plants.

SIZE
63cm/25in

SITE
East- or west-facing window

Zantedeschia hybrids
Arum lily

Zantedeschias do not flower for long periods, but the brevity of the display is well compensated for by the beauty and elegance of the flowers. There is a wide range of colours available, from rich orangey-yellow to purple, pink, and white. The flowering season runs from early- to midsummer after which plants die back for a dormant period. You can bring them back into growth during winter or early spring, ready to flower again. Alternatively, flowering plants can be used for a short term display and then discarded.

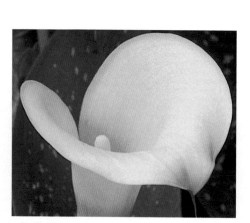

Z. elliottiana

HOW MUCH LIGHT
When the plant is in leaf provide bright light, including 1–2 hours of direct sunlight.

ROOM TEMPERATURE
Best at normal temperature 18–24°C (64–75°F): the flowers last longer in cooler conditions around 16°C (61°F).

WHEN TO WATER
Keep moist when in active growth but after flowering allow to dry out. Apply a balanced liquid feed fortnightly when plants are in full leaf and active growth.

SURVIVAL STRATEGY
Gradually dry off the plant after flowering, remove the collapsing leaves, and keep the dormant rhizome dry. Repot when new shoots emerge through the compost in winter or early spring, and gradually increase watering as leaves develop.

SIZE
50cm/20in

SITE
Conservatory

Plant care

Plantcare | Potting up

As plants get bigger, the roots become congested and may eventually need a bigger pot with more compost to satisfy their need for water and nutrients. Equally you may just want to move your plant into a more attractive container. Potting up to a larger size is a simple task if you follow a few basic rules about drainage and compost. Don't be tempted to pot into a vastly bigger container, as waterlogging may result.

Choosing compost

Most plants are happy in sterile, multi-purpose compost (don't use garden soil). Special composts are available for plants with particular needs: fast-draining and gritty for cacti; ericaceous for lime-haters, like camellias; and very coarse-textured compost for plants that dislike wet roots at any time, like orchids.

Adding extra nutrients

Multi-purpose composts have a limited supply of nutrients which are soon exhausted. Repotting provides the ideal opportunity to give the compost a boost by mixing fertiliser granules into the fresh compost. Through the effects of water and temperature, the granules release a steady supply of food to your plant over the whole growing season. Fertilisers come in several different forms but basically work the same way.

Granules should simply be mixed evenly into the compost.

Moisture-retentive multi-purpose compost

Sticks of fertiliser (above left) and clusters of granules (above), may be pressed into the compost surface (left). They gradually release their nutrients over several months; every time you water the plant the roots receive a boost, and old compost is revitalised.

Grity, open cacti compost.

Coarse, low nutrient orchid compost

How to pot up your plant

Repotting gives plants a new lease of life and encourages new healthy shoots. Use a pot just 2–3cm (1in) wider than the old one. Ideally repot your plant at the start of the growing season or when the plant is in active growth. Avoid repotting when the plant is dormant in winter as damaged roots may rot on inactive plants.

1 A 2–3cm (1in) layer of polystyrene pieces, broken pots or crockery across the hole provides necessary spaces for good drainage, and helps prevent waterlogging.

2cm (1in) allowed for watering

Rootball sits on a layer of compost

Polystyrene

2 Put a layer of compost in the bottom of the pot to bring the top of the rootball 2–3cm (1in) below the rim. This will provide just enough space for watering.

3 Carefully feed in the compost around the plant. Firm it in gently, but avoid over-compacting the compost as this hinders drainage and drives out all the air.

Layer of mulch

Compost fills sides

4 Add a layer of mulch for an attractive finish. It reduces evaporation, but makes checking for water more difficult. You'll need to scrape it away from the compost to check moisture levels.

Top-dressing

Plants in large pots are often too large or heavy to remove for repotting and may already be in as big a pot as you want. To keep them healthy apply a top-dressing of fresh compost each year in spring.

1 Remove the top 2–3cm (1in) of compost. Do not worry unduly about damaging fine roots.

2 Spread a 2–3cm (1in) layer of moist compost mixed with fertiliser over the surface.

Plantcare | Where to put your plant

The best way to ensure your plant stays healthy and performs well is to match its needs to a suitable position in your home. A plant may be aesthetically pleasing in a certain spot, but if the light and temperature conditions are inappropriate, and if you fail to meet other specific needs, such as humidity, it will soon lose its appeal as it becomes more and more sickly looking.

Effect of temperature

You are very unlikely to maintain a constant temperature in every part of your house. Cold draughts may blast through windows or doors that are regularly opened; an unheated spare room may provide relative winter cool; and an unventilated conservatory may experience blistering summer heat. In every case an awareness of the conditions will help you choose suitable plants.

Cacti are very robust. A resistance to hot days and cold nights means they are able to take fluctuating conservatory conditions.

Plants behind drawn curtains in winter can get caught in a trap of cold air. Avoid excluding them from a heated room.

Ways to increase humidity

Humidity refers to the amount of water in the air. The levels experienced by plants in their habitats often govern their needs: keep a plant from the tropical forest in dry air and its leaves will shrivel. Given too much humidity, plants from dry climates are likely to rot. Most houseplants are pretty tolerant, and you'll only need to raise humidity levels when it's hot to prevent plant stress.

The bathroom is often the most humid room in the house, due to hot baths or steamy showers. It's the ideal place for plants that demand higher humidity.

Plants give off moisture as part of their natural processes, so a group of plants creates a small area of higher humidity.

Mist leaves with water

Pebble layer is ideally as wide as the plant's spread

Keep water level just below the top of the pebbles

Stand a plant on a tray of moist pebbles to raise humidity through evaporation. Misting increases humidity, but you'll have to do it several times a day for it to be effective.

How much light?

Plant labels usually indicate the need for "direct", "bright filtered" or "medium" light, but what exactly does this mean? Light varies within the room, and at different times of year: plants unable to cope with hot direct summer sun may benefit from a site nearer the window in winter to better absorb weaker light. Plants need light to survive and naturally turn towards it; although twisting plants round every few days prevents lopsided growth it is not ideal, and some may suffer bud drop if the angle changes. It's best to ensure plants are correctly lit.

Plants in poor light may lean disfiguringly towards it; turn them to ensure even growth.

Direct light: the plant receives full sun for much of the day. Strong summer sun, especially at midday, is too much for most plants.

Bright, filtered light: sunlight through a net curtain or gauze blind remains bright but is far less likely to scorch the leaves of your plant.

Medium light: a position further into the room, away from the glare of a window suits many foliage plants which enjoy good light.

Low light: few plants enjoy the shady conditions where there is no direct source of light: those with large, dark green leaves are most likely to cope.

Boosting light levels

You can increase the amount of light available in rooms with little or no direct sun. Light, reflective walls and surfaces as well as paler-coloured furnishings will help to brighten a room. Keep the curtains drawn well back to allow as much light in as possible, and make sure your windows are clean. Consider whitewashing exterior garden walls close to the house to bounce light into the room.

Keep leaves clean to allow maximum light penetration. Use a soft damp cloth to remove grime or wash dirt away in a tepid shower.

Cacti look scruffy when covered in dust, which also blocks out much needed light. Clean between the spines safely with a paintbrush or cotton bud.

Plantcare | Food and water

Incorrect watering is probably the most common reason behind the untimely demise of a lot of houseplants. Just like humans, if you give them too much you can drown them; but if you don't provide enough then they'll die of thirst. Take the trouble to work out when your plants are ready for a drink, and how much they like and you should get along fine.

Watering from above

This is often the most convenient way to water, and is suitable for the majority of plants, particularly those with woody stems. It ensures the compost is evenly moist as water is drawn down by gravity. Ensure there is a 2–3cm (1in) gap between the compost surface and the lip of the pot: this allows space for a good dose of water, and you won't have to wait while it soaks in. Make sure that plants do not stand in excess water.

When to water

Check regularly and you'll learn that some plants dry out quicker than others. Large leafy plants and those in direct sun are usually among the first. Plants in terracotta pots dry quicker than those in glazed or plastic pots. Do not be tempted to water everything just because you have the watering can out: only water plants that need it – most are ready when the top 1cm (½in) is dry.

Press your fingers into the compost surface to find out how moist it is – scrape away a section of any mulch so that you can test the compost. As you become more familiar with the plants, you may be able to tell how dry they are by lifting them and judging their weight.

Watering from below

Plants with congested and fleshy stems such as African violets (*Saintpaulia*), pepperomias and cyclamen are prone to rotting in the centre if the plant becomes wet, so it is important to water these plants from below. You can also use this method to apply liquid feed. If there is layer of drainage material in the base of the pot you will need to use a deep saucer or bowl to ensure water reaches the roots. Most plants need about 20 minutes soaking time.

1 Pour water into the saucer to avoid wetting the crown of the plant, and leave the roots to soak up as much liquid as they need.

2 After about 20 minutes, drain away any water that remains in the saucer. Do not allow the plant to stand in water permanently.

Dunk and drain

Orchids are grown in loose, open compost and it is often difficult to tell when they are ready for a drink. These plants need careful handling because they are prone to damage from over-watering. As a rule of thumb, give them a weekly dunk in a bowl of tepid water. This allows the compost to absorb just enough water while you avoid the risk of giving them too much.

1 Remove the cachepot (if you have one). Carefully place the plant, still in its pot, in a bowl of soft water at room temperature, and leave it to stand for around 10 minutes.

2 Take the plant out of the bowl, and leave it to drain thoroughly – for about 30 minutes – before returning it to its cachepot and putting the plant back on display.

Special treatment

Epiphytic plants – those that grow in trees – often have poorly developed roots whose main purpose is anchorage. These plants acquire most of the water and nutrients that they need through their leaves rather than from their roots, and some have evolved to catch water in their vase-like rosettes.

A spray of soft water on plants like Tillandsia cynaea provides all the water they need. Add a quarter-strength liquid feed every month.

Fill the centre of rosette-forming bromeliads like aechmeas and vrieseas with soft water to supplement the water taken up by the roots.

Liquid feeds

Plants benefit greatly from regular feeding. This will usually be necessary a few weeks after you have bought your plant. Athough you can mix controlled-release fertilisers into the compost (*see p.176*), you will probably find it more convenient to provide a diluted feed at regular intervals when you water. A balanced liquid feed, at full or half-strength, will satisfy most plants, but there are special formulas available to satisfy the particular needs of orchids, citrus, ericaceous (lime-hating) plants, and foliage plants.

Some liquid feeds come in powder form. Simply follow the manufacturer's instructions, and dissolve the required amount in water.

Liquid formulations are very easy to make up. Measure out the amount of water, add a few drops and apply it with a watering can.

Plantcare | Watering problems

Watering seems to cause a disproportionate amount of angst. We fret if we forget to water plants and worry when they wilt, or strive to do the right thing and end up over-watering – which, because it kills the roots, also makes plants wilt. Drought is fairly obvious as the compost is dry, but wilting due to over-watering is more insidious: continually wet compost slowly destroys the roots. Over-watered plants can be revived, but you'll also need to give them some TLC.

Drying out plants

If you find you have over-watered your plant, all is not lost: it may be possible to dry it out. Remove the pot and wrap the rootball with paper towels or newspaper until all the excess moisture has been drawn out of the compost. Then keep it only just moist and out of direct sun for a few weeks while the roots recover.

This begonia has been neglected for too long, and its drooping leaves obviously indicate a need for water. Given a drink and kept out of the sun it will perk up within an hour.

Reviving a wilted plant

The effects of underwatering can look dramatic: a plant may quite suddenly appear to collapse overnight and greet you with limp, wilted stems drooping sadly over the sides of its pot the next day. Compost that is too dry shrinks away from the sides of the pot, and allows water to pass straight through it when you attempt to rehydrate it by watering normally.

1 When confronted with a wilted plant, before you take any action, be sure to check that dry compost is the problem. Confusingly, wilting may be due to over-watering, or vine weevil damage.

2 Move it to a cool area out of direct sun and place the plastic pot in a bowl of tepid water. If the rootball is so dry that it floats, weigh it down with a pebble on the compost surface..

3 After soaking for about 20 minutes remove the bowl and let the pot drain for 10 minutes before replacing the cachepot. The plant should show signs of recovery within about an hour.

Holiday watering

What to do with plants when you go on holiday? If you have a willing neighbour, all's well and good (but if you worry that a well-intentioned neighbour, keen not to let the plants die of drought, may over-water them instead, then set up reservoirs or capillary systems and ask them to top up the water levels). Plants can usually cope without you for a long weekend: water them well before you go and move them to a cool room out of the sun. If it's practical, put them all in the bath and water them there. Some pots have a "self-watering" device – little more than a reservoir of water below the plant into which the roots grow – but your plant must already be established in such a pot for it to be of use.

A capillary watering system can be simple to set up and, depending on their size, may be enough to see your plants through a week's holiday. Put the plug in, and place capillary matting (or a towel) over the kitchen drainer and along the bottom of the sink. Stand your plants on top of the matting on the drainer. Moisture travels up the matting, and spreads to the base of the pots where it is absorbed by the compost. This method is not suitable for pots with crocks or drainage material in the base as the mat must be in contact with the compost – and of course, any cachepots must be removed. If possible do a test run for a day: this allows you to gauge how long a full sink will last, and check the plug does not leak.

A wick system may suit plants that are too big to move. Put a bowl of water above the level of the compost, weigh down a strip of capillary matting with a pebble, and press the other end into the compost.

Create a large reservoir which drips water into the compost via a hole in the cap by cutting the base off a plastic bottle. Only a tiny hole is needed in the bottle top. It is wise to experiment before you go away.

Plantcare | On-growing support

Properly cared for, plants are going to grow – some very vigorously – and sooner or later they will need your help to keep them looking good or within bounds. Time trimming or training is rewarded with shapely plants, and a greater understanding of how they grow.

How to train up a moss pole

Moss poles are ideal for climbers like cheese plants (*Monstera*). You can either buy them, or make your own by wrapping moss around a plastic tube and binding it with fishing line. Keep it moist to encourage ariel roots to penetrate the moss.

1 It's easy to tame a wayward monstera upwards. Using a spoon handle, make a small hole in the compost, avoiding major roots, and push pole firmly into the pot.

2 Although it seems a tangled mess, this plant has two main stems. Gently twist each stem around the pole in turn, taking care not to break them.

3 Keep stems in contact with the pole as much as possible and tie them in with soft garden twine. Use a shoelace knot that is easy to adjust as you manoeuvre stems.

4 Step back regularly to check your work as you tie in the stems to be sure the plant is well balanced – it not only looks good but makes the finished plant stable.

Making loops

Most trailing or climbing plants can be "formalised" on a frame to give them an entirely new look. Here I have used a bushy trailing ivy, but plants like jasmine, passion flower, cissus or even *Tradescantia zebrina* can be treated this way.

1 Provide a suitably-sized circle of stout wire, ideally galvanised or coated, leaving two long straight "legs" on the end, and push them down into the compost just inside the rim of the pot.

2 Taking the longest stems first, wind them around the wire from both ends of the loop. Gradually weave other stems into the loop to create a robust-looking circle of greenery.

3 Once you are happy with the overall effect, trim off all the other trailing shoots. Keep it neat and tidy by clipping over with scissors or secateurs and bending new shoots into the loop.

Keeping plants in trim

As plants develop they may lose their shape, and in the case of climbers, they can start to grow away from their supports. Keep on top of tweaking, trimming, and tying-in shoots to ensure your plants continue looking at their best.

Many climbers like this passion flower make vigorous growth but you can contain them by training new shoots back along themselves on the framework. It's best to do this while the shoots are young and pliable. Occasionally cutting out old shoots is a job that will test your patience but it helps to maintain your plant's youth and vigour.

Formal shapes need regular clipping. On foliage plants this is straightforward as most can be cut back at any time during their growing period. With flowering plants, if you are unsure it's best to wait until flowering is over before cutting back. This olive is being pruned when it is easy to see where the flowers are.

Deadheading

Many plants stop flowering once they have set seed which means removing spent blooms encourages new buds to form. Plants with large flowers like this hibiscus look tidier with old flowers removed, and this also prevents fallen petals resting on and rotting the foliage. Cut off as much of the flower stalk as possible to prevent rotting.

Creating a standard

Growing a plant on a single stem can give it a completely new character and adds another dimension to plant groupings. Here I have used an abutilon but you can achieve the same effect with lantana, pachira, citrus or, with extra support, ivy.

1 Choose a plant with a strong, centrally-placed and unbranching stem that runs right to the top of the plant to train as a standard.

2 Cut out any competing upright shoots then remove the leaves and any sideshoots from the lower half of the plant.

3 Thin stems need support. Avoid "throttling" the stem by tying string around the cane first and then loosely round the stem.

4 When plant reaches the desired height, pinch out the leading tip for a bushy head. Rub off any young shoots that sprout on the bare stem.

Plantcare | What's gone wrong?

There are three main causes of ill-health in plants: pests and diseases, incorrect watering, and poor siting. The problem is that plants often react in similar ways to all these events with yellowing or browning leaves, wilting stems, or by shedding flowers and foliage. So how do you know what's gone wrong? The first thing to remember is: Don't Panic. Avoid jumping to conclusions, learn to read your plants, and try to work out what's really bothering them. In the case of pests and diseases, your best defence is to exercise vigilance, and deal with trouble before it gets out of hand.

Poor begonia. Lack of food has turned foliage yellow. Debris and old leaves have been left to rot on the compost. Rot has spread to the stems causing more die-back. Underwatering has made it wilt.

Yellowing leaves

• A sign of age
Low leaves often turn yellow and drop off as plants grow: they are shed as they are inefficient.
DON'T WORRY, this is natural. Remove old leaves as they fade to keep the plant looking tidy.

• Low temperatures
Plants accustomed to warmth may become stressed if temperatures fall. This causes leaves to yellow, and may be accompanied by brown spots.
MOVE PLANTS to a warmer environment to recover.

• Under-nourishment
Nitrogen is essential to produce chlorophyll. If compost fails to provide enough nitrogen, plants are unable to make chlorophyll or collect light energy. Plants short of nitrogen move it to where it is needed most, often the top of the plant, causing lower leaves to fade.
REGULAR FEEDING with a balanced fertiliser prevents poor nutrition.

• Hard water
Some plants need lime-free conditions. Hard water raises the compost's lime content making iron and nitrogen unavailable.
USE SOFT WATER and a feed formulated for lime-hating plants.

• Underwatering
Plants kept dry cannot take up water and fail to get the nutrients water brings leading to under-nourishment and yellow lower leaves.
CHECK REGULARLY for dry compost and water accordingly.

• Overwatering
Waterlogged roots cannot function properly and do not provide plants with essential water or nutrients so the leaves yellow and stems wilt despite the compost being moist.
DO NOT LEAVE plants standing in water-filled saucers. See p.182.

Leaf, flower, or bud drop

• Sudden temperature changes
These can shock plants into shedding buds and leaves to conserve energy.
PROVIDE more stable conditions

• The angle of light has changed
As plants adjust to the new light source buds become detached.
AVOID turning these plants and ensure they are correctly lit.

• Under-watering
The plant sheds leaves and buds to conserve moisture.
CHECK compost and water plant.

Scorched leaves

• Too much heat
Hot conditions especially when combined with inadequate water cause scorched leaves.
REDUCE temperature, increase watering, and raise humidity.

• Not enough humidity
Leaves lose water faster than it travels into the leaf, causing their tips and edges to dry out and turn brown.
MOVE PLANTS to a more humid area or mist to raise humidity.

Pests and diseases

Adult vine weevils are slow, flightless creatures that come out at night and chew notches in leaf margins. They are easily caught and picked off.

Vine weevil grubs eat away at plant roots unnoticed until the plant wilts. Chemical or biological nematode controls are available

Soft, crowded, damaged, or over-wet plant tissue is at risk from attacks of grey mould. Prevent by removing fallen leaves and practice good hygiene.

Red spider mites are tiny but speckling and webbing on leaves indicate their presence. Use biological and chemical controls.

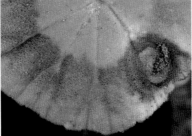

Fallen petals left lying on foliage cause moulds to develop. Pelargoniums are particularly prone to this problem. Deadhead regularly.

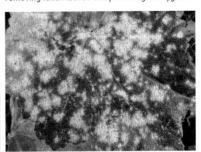

Powdery mildew is generally a begonia problem and only on plants stressed by drought or heat. Improve conditions and spray with fungicide.

Aphids increase rapidly in warm conditions. Rub them off or use chemical and biological controls.

Mealy bugs hide in leaves and stems. Rub them off, dig them out or use biological controls.

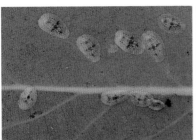

Soft scale insects are easily spotted on stems and leaves. Rub off or use biological controls.

Whitefly. Best controlled with biological controls or chemicals to kill all stages of their lifecycle.

Sooty mould is nature's way of telling you have a problem with aphids, scale insects, whitefly or mealy bugs, all of which exude a sticky waste on which the mould grows. Cure your insect problem and you cure your sooty mould problem.

Index | Plant categories

This list is intended as a guide to help you find an appropriate plant for your site, or one with particular characteristics.

DRAMATIC SHAPE

FLOWERS

LARGE PLANTS

Index | Plant categories

Index | Common names

Acknowledgements

AUTHOR'S ACKNOWLEDGEMENTS
A very big thank you to Kate Kenyan at the Flowers and Plants Association whose help and cooperation in locating, collecting and delivering plants was massive and made life so much easier.

An extremely big and special thanks to the DK team of Helen Fewster and Rachael Smith whose professionalism has made the whole project run smoothly and efficiently and, best of all, it has always been done with a smile.

Big thanks also to Sian Irvine for her hospitality and chocolate biscuits.

Many thanks to Fibrex Nursery, Pebworth, Warwickshire for help identifying Pelargonium cultivars. Thank you also to Gwen Dixon for the loan of plant material.

The publishers also wish to thank Ali Edney and Juliette Hopkins.

Thanks also to: Crocus.co.uk; The Chelsea Gardener; R.K. Alliston; and Marston & Langinger, 192 Ebury Street, London, SW1W 8UP (+44 020 7881 5717) for the loan of their pots.

PHOTOGRAPHY CREDITS
The publisher would like to thank the following for their kind permission to reproduce their photographs:

Abbreviations key: a=above, b=below, c=centre, l=left; r=right, t=top
Alamy Images: Holt Studios International Ltd 187tr, 187ca, 187cra.
Ardea.com: Steve Hopkin 187tl.
Photos Horticultural: 187cla, 187br; B.T. 187clb.

COMMISSIONED PHOTOGRAPHS
Craig Knowles: 165 inset, 167 inset, 181 bl, 181 bc.
Verity Welstead: 15, 60, 61l, 61tr, 89bl, 103t, 116, 117tr, 131tl, 145tr, 176tc, 179c, 179cr.
All other images © Dorling Kindersley
For further information see:
www.dkimages.com